OFFICIAL SQA PAST PAPERS WITH ANSWERS

STANDARD GRADE | GENERAL | CREDIT

ENGLISH
2006-2009

SQA

BrightRED
PUBLISHING

© Scottish Qualifications Authority

First exam published in 2006.
Published by Bright Red Publishing Ltd, 6 Stafford Street, Edinburgh EH3 7AU
tel: 0131 220 5804 fax: 0131 220 6710 info@brightredpublishing.co.uk www.brightredpublishing.co.uk

ISBN 978-1-84948-011-6

A CIP Catalogue record for this book is available from the British Library.

Bright Red Publishing is grateful to the copyright holders, as credited on the final page of the book, for permission to use their material. Every effort has been made to trace the copyright holders and to obtain their permission for the use of copyright material. Bright Red Publishing will be happy to receive information allowing us to rectify any error or omission in future editions.

STANDARD GRADE | GENERAL

2006
READING

[BLANK PAGE]

G

0860/403

NATIONAL
QUALIFICATIONS
2006

WEDNESDAY, 3 MAY
1.00 PM – 1.50 PM

ENGLISH
STANDARD GRADE
General Level
Reading
Text

Read carefully the passage overleaf. It will help if you read it twice. When you have done so, answer the questions. Use the spaces provided in the Question/Answer booklet.

SCOTTISH
QUALIFICATIONS
AUTHORITY

In this extract from a novel set in a secondary school, the narrator, John, is sitting in his Maths class. Gloria (nicknamed Glory Hallelujah) is another pupil in the same class.

1   I am sitting in school, in Maths, with a piece of paper in my hand. No, it is not my algebra homework. It is not a quiz that I have finished and am waiting to hand in to Mrs Moonface. The piece of paper in my hand has nothing at all to do with Mathematics. Nor does it have to do with any school subject. Nor is it really a piece of paper at all.

2   It is really my fate, masquerading as paper.

3   I am sitting next to Glory Hallelujah and I am waiting for a break in the action. Mrs Moonface is at the front of the room, going on about integers. I am not hearing a single thing that she is saying. She could stop lecturing about integers and start doing a cancan kick or singing a rap song and I would not notice.

4   She could call on me and ask me any question on earth, and I would not be able to answer.

5   But luckily, she does not call on me. She has a piece of chalk in her right hand. She is waving it around like a dagger as she spews algebra gibberish at a hundred miles a minute.

6   I hear nothing. Algebra does not have the power to penetrate my feverish isolation.

7   You see, I am preparing to ask Glory Hallelujah out on a date.

8   I am on an island, even though I am sitting at my desk surrounded by my classmates.

9   I am on Torture Island.

10   There are no trees on Torture Island—no huts, no hills, no beaches. There is only doubt.

11   Gloria will laugh at me. That thought is my lonely and tormenting company here on Torture Island. The exact timing and nature of her laughter are open to endless speculation.

12   She may not take me seriously. Her response may be "Oh, John, do you exist? Are you here on earth with me? I wasn't aware we were sharing the same universe."

13   Or she may be even more sarcastic. "John, I would love to go on a date with you, but I'm afraid I have to change my cat's litter box that night ."

14   So, as you can see, Torture Island is not exactly a beach resort. I am not having much fun here. I am ready to seize my moment and leave Torture Island forever.

15   In registration, I ripped a piece of paper from my yellow notepad. My black ball-point pen shook slightly in my trembling right hand as I wrote out the fateful question: "Gloria, will you go out with me this Friday?" Beneath that monumental question, I drew two boxes. One box was conspicuously large. I labelled it the YES box. The second box was tiny. I labelled it the NO box.

16   And that is the yellow piece of paper I have folded up into a square and am holding in my damp hand as I wait here on Torture Island for Mrs Moonface to turn towards the blackboard and give me the opportunity I need.

17   I cannot approach Glory Hallelujah after class because she is always surrounded by her friends. I cannot wait and pass the note to her later in the week because she may make plans to go out with one of her girlfriends. No, it is very evident to me that today is the day, and that I must pass the note before this period ends or forever live a coward.

18   There are only ten minutes left in Maths and Mrs Moonface seems to have no intention of recording her algebraic observations for posterity. Perhaps the piece of yellow chalk in her hand is just a prop. It is possible that the previous night she hurt her wrist in an arm-wrestling competition and can no longer write. It is also possible that she has forgotten all about her pupils and believes that she is playing a part in a Hollywood movie.

19   There are only seven minutes left in Maths. I attempt to turn Mrs Moonface towards the blackboard by telekinesis. The atoms of her body prove remarkably resistant to my telepathic powers.

20   There are six minutes left. Now there are five.

21   Mrs Moonface, for Pete's sake, write something on the blackboard! That is what Mathematics teachers do! Write down axioms, simplify equations, draw rectangles, measure angles, even, if you must, sketch the sneering razor-toothed face of Algebra itself. WRITE ANYTHING!

22   Suddenly Mrs Moonface stops lecturing.

23   Her right hand, holding the chalk, rises.

24   Then her hips begin to pivot.

25   This all unfolds in very slow motion. The sheer importance of the moment slows the action way, way down.

26   The pivoting of Mrs Moonface's hips causes a corresponding rotation in the plane of her shoulders and upper torso.

27   Her neck follows her shoulders, as day follows night.

28   Eventually, the lunar surface of her face is pulled towards the blackboard.

29   She begins to write. I have no idea what she is writing. It could be hieroglyphics and I would not notice. It could be a map to Blackbeard's treasure and I would not care.

30   I am now primed. My heart is thumping against my ribs, one by one, like a hammer pounding out a musical scale on a metal keyboard. Bing. Bang. Bong. Bam. I am breathing so quickly that I cannot breathe, if that makes any sense.

31   I am aware of every single one of my classmates in Maths.

32   Everyone in Maths is now preoccupied. There are only four minutes left in the period. Mrs Moonface is filling up blackboard space at an unprecedented speed, no doubt trying to scrape every last kernel of mathematical knowledge from the corncob of her brain before the bell. My classmates are racing to keep up with her. All around me pens are moving across notebooks at such a rate that ink can barely leak out and affix itself to paper.

33   My moment is at hand! The great clapper in the bell of fate clangs for me! *Ka-wang! Ka-wang!*

34   My right hand rises and begins to move sideways, very slowly, like a submarine, travelling at sub-desk depth to avoid teacher radar.

35   My right index finger makes contact with the sacred warm left wrist of Glory Hallelujah!

36   She looks down to see who is touching her at sub-desk depth. Spots my hand, with its precious yellow note.

37   Gloria understands instantly.

38   The exchange of the covert note is completed in a nanoinstant. Mrs Moonface and the rest of our Maths class have no idea that anything momentous has taken place.

39   I reverse the speed and direction of my right hand, and it returns safely to port.

40   Gloria has transferred my note to her lap and has moved her right elbow to block anyone on that side of her from seeing. The desk itself provides added shielding.

41   In the clever safe haven that she has created, she unfolds my note. Reads it.

42   She does not need to speak. She does not need to check the YES or NO boxes on my note. If she merely blinks, I will understand. If she wrinkles her nose, the import of her nose wrinkle will not be lost on me. In fact, so total is my concentration in that moment of grand suspense I am absolutely positive that there is nothing that Glory Hallelujah can do, no reaction that she can give off, that I will not immediately and fully understand.

43   I would stake my life on it.

44   But what she does do is this. She folds my note back up. Without looking at me—without even an eye blink or a nose wrinkle—she raises it to her lips. For one wild instant I think that she is going to kiss it.

45   Her pearly teeth part.

46   She eats my note.

Adapted from the novel *"You Dont Know Me"* By David Klass

[*END OF PASSAGE*]

FOR OFFICIAL USE

G

Total Mark

0860/404

NATIONAL
QUALIFICATIONS
2006

WEDNESDAY, 3 MAY
1.00 PM – 1.50 PM

**ENGLISH
STANDARD GRADE**
General Level
Reading
Questions

Fill in these boxes and read what is printed below.

Full name of centre

Town

Forename(s)

Surname

Date of birth
  Day Month Year

Scottish candidate number

Number of seat

**NB Before leaving the examination room you must give this booklet to the invigilator.
If you do not, you may lose all the marks for this paper.**

SCOTTISH
QUALIFICATIONS
AUTHORITY

©

Marks

QUESTIONS

Write your answers in the spaces provided.

Look at Paragraphs 1 to 4.

1. (*a*) Who is Mrs Moonface?

    _____   2 ■ 0

    (*b*) Why do you think John gives her the nickname "Mrs Moonface"?

    _____

    _____   2 1 0

2. "It is really my fate, masquerading as paper."

    Why does the writer place this sentence in a paragraph of its own?

    _____

    _____   2 1 0

3. "Mrs Moonface is at the front of the room, going on about integers."

    What does the expression "going on" suggest about John's attitude to what Mrs Moonface is saying?

    _____   2 ■ 0

Look at Paragraphs 5 to 10.

4. How does the writer make Mrs Moonface's behaviour seem threatening?

    _____

    _____   2 1 0

PAGE
TOTAL

Marks

5. ". . . spews algebra gibberish at a hundred miles a minute. . ." (Paragraph 5)

Explain in your own words what the writer's word choice in this expression suggests about what John thinks of:

(i) **what** she is saying

_____

_____   2 ■ 0

(ii) **how** she says it

_____

_____   2 ■ 0

6. ". . . I am preparing to ask Glory Hallelujah out on a date." (Paragraph 7)

Why do you think the writer waits until this point to reveal what John is planning to do?

_____

_____   2 1 0

7. "I am on Torture Island." (Paragraph 9)

(*a*) **Explain fully in your own words** what the narrator means by this.

_____

_____   2 1 0

(*b*) Write down an expression from later in the passage which contains a similar idea.

+---+
| |
+---+   2 ■ 0

[Turn over

PAGE
TOTAL

Marks

8. Explain how the writer emphasises the bleakness of "Torture Island".

_____

_____   2   1   0

Look at Paragraphs 11 to 14.

9. (*a*) **Write down an example** of the writer's use of humour in these paragraphs.

_____

_____   2 ■ 0

(*b*) Explain why your chosen example is funny.

_____

_____   2   1   0

Look at Paragraphs 15 to 17.

10. Write down three pieces of evidence that suggest the narrator's nervousness at this point in the story.

_____

_____

_____   2   1   0

11. Quote **two** separate words used by the writer to suggest the importance of what John is asking Gloria.

[   ]   [   ]   2   1   0

12. "One box was conspicuously large . . . The second box was tiny." (Paragraph 15)

Why do you think John makes the boxes different sizes?

_____

_____   2   1   0

PAGE
TOTAL

Marks

13. **In your own words**, give a reason why John must make his approach to Gloria during Maths.

_____

_____ | 2 | 1 | 0

Look at Paragraphs 18 to 21.

14. How does the writer suggest the mood of increasing tension at this point in the passage?

_____

_____ | 2 | ■ | 0

15. "WRITE ANYTHING!" (Paragraph 21)

Why are these words written in capital letters?

_____

_____ | 2 | ■ | 0

Look at Paragraphs 22 to 33

16. (*a*) Identify any **one** technique used by the writer in this section to suggest John's growing excitement.

_____ | 2 | ■ | 0

(*b*) Explain **how** it does so.

_____

_____ | 2 | 1 | 0

[Turn over for Questions 17 to 20 on *Page six*

PAGE
TOTAL

Marks

Look at Paragraphs 34 to 46.

17. Give **three** reasons why Mrs Moonface is unaware of the note being passed.

_____

_____

_____   2 1 0

18. Why does John feel the "YES" or "NO" boxes on his note are now irrelevant?

_____

_____   2 1 0

19. How does the final paragraph provide an effective end to the passage?

_____

_____   2 1 0

Now look at the passage as a whole.

20. How realistic do you find the writer's description of this classroom incident? Give reasons for your opinion.

_____

_____

_____   2 1 0

[END OF QUESTION PAPER]

PAGE TOTAL

STANDARD GRADE | CREDIT

2006
READING

[BLANK PAGE]

C

0860/405

NATIONAL
QUALIFICATIONS
2006

WEDNESDAY, 3 MAY
2.30 PM – 3.20 PM

ENGLISH
STANDARD GRADE
Credit Level
Reading
Text

Read carefully the passage overleaf. It will help if you read it twice. When you have done so, answer the questions. Use the spaces provided in the Question/Answer booklet.

SCOTTISH
QUALIFICATIONS
AUTHORITY

Casting a spell all over America

It's broadcast live on television and nine million children take part. **Alex Massie** gets out his dictionary and enters the world of the spelling bee.

1 Askay Buddiga had prepared thoroughly for this moment. The 13-year-old from Colorado Springs knew what was required of him. After all, his brother had won the Scripps Howard National Spelling Bee just two years earlier, and now he was here at the final. Perhaps the pressure of family expectation got to him for a moment. Perhaps he panicked.

2 Whatever the reason, when pronouncer Dr Jacques Bailly announced that the teenager's word in the sixth round of the competition was "alopecoid", Buddiga suddenly collapsed. The 1,000-strong audience gathered at the Hyatt hotel in downtown Washington DC was stunned. He had fainted.

3 But within 30 seconds he was back on his feet—calmly spelling a-l-o-p-e-c-o-i-d to much applause. Buddiga recovered sufficiently to go on to the final rounds of the competition.

4 Though it might seem arcane in the age of computer spellcheck programs, more than nine million American children took part in spelling contests this year, with the top 265 progressing to Washington for the grand finals last week.

5 With yellow numbered ID placards hung around their necks, the contestants looked as if they had been summoned to take part in a police line-up. One by one the youngsters stepped up to the microphone to hear and spell their words. Although they operated on a two-minute time limit, they could ask for alternative pronunciations, the definition and derivation of the word and ask for it to be used in a sentence. A contestant might be asked to spell such words as "widdershins", "hauberk", "putrescible", "gallimaufry" and "salicylate".

6 But the competition really got going when the field was whittled down to the final two dozen spellers on day three. By then, contestants were beginning to struggle as they tiptoed, letter by letter, through their words as though they were crossing a minefield. "Vimineous" ended North Carolina's Simon Winchester challenge.

"Parrhesia" did the same for Nichols James Truelson, who slumped back into his chair with a bemused, vacant look on his face as the audience applauded sympathetically. But the greatest ovation was reserved for Buddiga, who eventually stumbled on "schwarmerei", but still managed to finish runner-up.

7 The bee is televised live and makes for oddly gripping television. The merciless nature of the competition, where a single misplaced consonant or forgotten vowel ejects a speller from the contest, gives proceedings a kind of high-wire drama as the spellers fret their way through the rounds, each more difficult than the last. It might seem an unlikely ratings success, but it certainly beats the world wood-chopping championships.

8 Some parents are tempted to take their child's preparation for the bee to extraordinary, obsessive lengths. It's a perennial cliché of American sportswriting but there's more than a hint of truth in the old phrase that in the land of the free, only winners are remembered.

9 And spelling is on the up. The remarkable success of the documentary *Spellbound*, which followed eight spellers to the bee and was nominated for an Academy Award last year, brought the competition to a new audience.

10 *Spellbound* featured one boy, Neil, whose father hired specialist tutors to coach his son in words derived from French and German. Despite such dedication, Neil didn't win.

11 But the proclivities of such contestants and their parents in no way represent the general participant. "It's not just the geeks and the nerds. These are normal kids," says Ohio's Beth Richards, whose daughter, Bailey, was making her second appearance in the finals. "This is the Superbowl of words."

12 While runner-up Buddiga sat quietly, hands in pockets and with the stern spelling equivalent of a poker face, his rival, 14-year-old David Tidmarsh from South Bend, Indiana, was running on nervous energy, fidgeting constantly and squinting into the

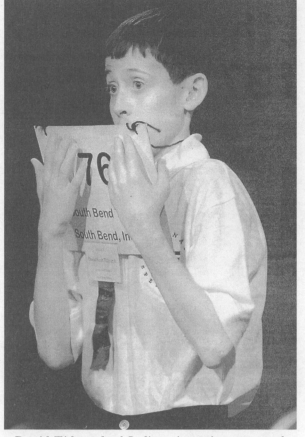

David Tidmarsh of Indiana just minutes away from winning the National Spelling Bee

distance as he worked out the correct spelling of the championship word. He would be champion if he could successfully spell "autochthonous" (meaning indigenous). "Could you use it in a sentence please?" he asked, as his voice rose an octave and he struggled to control his breathing.

13 He appeared close to hyperventilating as he started slowly then rattled through the word, confident that, after three days of ruthless competition, the grand prize was his. Blinking in amazement, he appeared overwhelmed, burying his face in his hands as his mother rushed the stage to embrace him. "It's kind of sad I won't be able to be in more spelling bees," says Tidmarsh. The tears welled in his eyes as he contemplated the awful void that lay ahead. Unlike boxers or basketball stars there's no second coming or return from retirement available to champion spellers. Former winners are not eligible to enter.

14 On the other hand, spellers leave on a high note and neither they nor their audience are likely to be humbled and saddened by the sight of an ageing champion dragging his weary body into the ring for one final ignominious battle against fresher faced opponents.

15 Tidmarsh's father Jay, a law professor, appeared almost as nervous as his son as he paced around the outer edge of the Hyatt hotel ballroom, unable to keep still or watch proceedings with equanimity. "I never actually thought about what it would be like to win. I guess I just couldn't believe it. It was just really surreal," says his son, after being presented with the trophy and cheques worth $17,000. "My parents will probably put it in a savings account," he adds, his voice tinged with resignation. "But I'll try and get hold of some of it to spend at the mall."

16 Tidmarsh was the first winner from Indiana since 1928 and his triumph was front page news and the subject of numerous editorials in his home state's newspapers. "It's this great slice of Americana," says the 1979 champion Katie Kerwin McCrimmon, who now commentates on the bee for television. "You come home, and there are banners at the airport and signs in the streets."

17 Robert Rappoport, from Albany, New York, whose son Paul was eliminated in the second round, says: "There are no second chances and only one winner. This is the real thing. There are only probably a few who are really in with a chance of winning and who become obsessed with the bee. Most of the competitors are just bright kids who like to read."

18 A cursory survey of the contestants' names—Chen, Srinivasan, Biedermann, Ofori, Milovac, Irwinsky, Menendez, McMahon— points to one reason for the bee's popularity. It is the personification of the American melting pot and gives substance to the American dream. If you want it enough and work hard enough you can succeed in America.

19 Outside the Hyatt Hotel a ragbag collection of protestors from the Simplified Spelling Society waving placards proclaiming "I'm thru with through" and "50,000,000 illiterates can't be wrong" pressed leaflets arguing for an overhaul of spelling upon dubious and somewhat nonplussed contestants.

20 For David Tidmarsh and his fellow contestants, however, there's nothing wrong with the language as it stands. During an impromptu press conference he was asked if all this was as good as Hollywood can make it.

21 The young champion thought for a second before a goofy grin spread across his face: "It's even better."

Adapted from an article in
The Scotsman

[*END OF PASSAGE*]

[BLANK PAGE]

C

FOR OFFICIAL USE

Total Mark

0860/406

NATIONAL
QUALIFICATIONS
2006

WEDNESDAY, 3 MAY
2.30 PM – 3.20 PM

ENGLISH
STANDARD GRADE
Credit Level
Reading
Questions

Fill in these boxes and read what is printed below.

Full name of centre

Town

Forename(s)

Surname

Date of birth
Day   Month   Year   Scottish candidate number   Number of seat

NB   Before leaving the examination room you must give this booklet to the invigilator. If you do not, you may lose all the marks for this paper.

SCOTTISH
QUALIFICATIONS
AUTHORITY

SAB 0860/406 6/00000

©

Marks

QUESTIONS

Write your answers in the spaces provided.

Look at Paragraphs 1 to 3.

1. (*a*)   In what sort of a contest is Askay Buddiga taking part?

_____   2 ■ 0

   (*b*)   Give **three** reasons why Askay might have expected to do well.

_____

_____

_____   2 1 0

2. "He had fainted." (Paragraph 2)

   How does the writer signal the dramatic nature of this event to the reader?

_____

_____   2 1 0

3. **In your own words**, what might have been the reasons for Askay's fainting?

_____

_____   2 1 0

4. "a-l-o-p-e-c-o-i-d" (Paragraph 3)

   Why does the writer separate the letters in this word with dashes?

_____   2 ■ 0

PAGE
TOTAL

Marks

Look at Paragraphs 4 to 6.

5. "Though it might seem arcane . . ." (Paragraph 4)

   Explain in your own words why spelling contests might seem "arcane" or strange.

   _____

   _____

   _____   2 1 0

6. ". . . contestants looked as though they had been summoned to take part in a police line-up." (Paragraph 5)

   What does this description suggest about how the contestants may have been feeling?

   _____   2 ■ 0

7. **In your own words**, explain what **four** things each contestant could ask for to help them with the spelling of a word.

   _____

   _____

   _____

   _____   2 1 0

[Turn over

PAGE
TOTAL

Marks

8. "as though they were crossing a minefield" (Paragraph 6)

(*a*) Identify the figure of speech the writer is using here.

_____   2 ■ 0

(*b*) **In your own words**, explain how appropriate you find the use of this image.

_____

_____   2 1

(*c*) Write down an expression used later in the passage which contains a similar idea to ". . . crossing a minefield".

_____

_____   2 ■ 0

Look at Paragraphs 8 to 11.

9. "Some parents are tempted to take their child's preparation for the bee to extraordinary, obsessive lengths." (Paragraph 8)

Give a reason why some parents are prepared to behave in this way.

_____

_____   2 ■ 0

10. How does the first sentence of Paragraph 11 act as a link between Paragraphs 10 and 11?

_____

_____

_____   2 1

Marks

Look at Paragraphs 12 to 15.

11. **In your own words**, explain fully the differing reactions of David Tidmarsh and Askay Buddiga in Paragraph 12.

    (i) **Buddiga:**

    _____

    _____   2 1 0

    (ii) **Tidmarsh:**

    _____

    _____   2 1 0

12. ". . . the awful void that lay ahead." (Paragraph 13)

    (*a*) What is the "awful void" that lies ahead of Tidmarsh?

    _____   2 ■ 0

    (*b*) What tone is the writer adopting in the expression?

    _____   2 ■ 0

13. "Former winners are not eligible to enter." (Paragraph 13)

    In your own words, explain how the writer illustrates the advantages of this rule in paragraph 14.

    _____

    _____   2 1 0

Look at Paragraphs 16 to 21.

14. "It's this great slice of Americana" (Paragraph 16)

    What do you think Katie Kerwin McCrimmon means by this?

    _____

    _____   2 1 0

[Turn over

PAGE TOTAL

Marks

15. "It is the personification of the American melting pot . . ." (Paragraph 18)

How does the writer illustrate this idea in Paragraph 18?

_____

_____　2　1

16. What does the writer's use of the words "ragbag collection" to describe the protestors suggest about his attitude towards them?

_____　2　■

17. "I'm thru with through" (Paragraph 19)

Explain the **two** different spellings of the word "through" on the protestors' placards.

_____

_____

_____　2　1

18. In your own words, explain the contestants' reaction to the protestors.

_____

_____　2　■

Think about the passage as a whole.

19. Quote **three** expressions from the passage which convey the view that the contestants are really no different from other children.

_____

_____

_____　2　1

PAGE
TOTAl

Marks

20. Why is "Casting a spell all over America" a good title for this article?

_____

_____

_____

2 1 0

[END OF QUESTION PAPER]

PAGE
TOTAL

FOR OFFICIAL USE

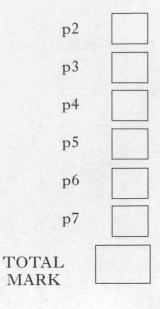

p2

p3

p4

p5

p6

p7

TOTAL
MARK

FOR OFFICIAL USE

[BLANK PAGE]

G

0860/403

NATIONAL
QUALIFICATIONS
2007

TUESDAY, 1 MAY
1.00 PM – 1.50 PM

ENGLISH
STANDARD GRADE
General Level
Reading
Text

Read carefully the passage overleaf. It will help if you read it twice. When you have done so, answer the questions. Use the spaces provided in the Question/Answer booklet.

SCOTTISH
QUALIFICATIONS
AUTHORITY

Biker Boys and Girls

There is only one "wall of death" doing the rounds at British fairs today. But a new generation of daredevil riders is intent on keeping the show on (or rather, off) the road.

1   Last year Kerri Cameron, aged 19 and a little bored with her job as a horse-riding instructor, was looking up job vacancies on the internet. Puzzled, she turned to her mother and said, "Mum, what's a wall of death?"

2   Her mother, Denise, a health worker who has always had a horror of motorcycles, told her that walls of death were places where people rode motorbikes round the insides of a 20 ft-high wooden drum and tried not to fall off and get killed. "Gosh," said Kerri, "that sounds fun."

3   She picked up her mobile, phoned the number mentioned on the internet and then arranged to see Ken Fox, owner of the wall of death. Ken Fox didn't ask about her school qualifications, only if she wanted a ride on the back of his bike around the wall. Yes, she said.

4   Ken Fox revved up the demonstration bike and spun it on to the 45-degree wooden apron that bridges the ground and the perpendicular wall and then took it three or four times around the lower bits of the wall itself just to see if she could cope. Then he went round with Kerri sitting on the handlebars. She passed that test, too. She thought it was fantastic. Unbelievable. The best!

5   A year later Kerri is doing 20 shows a day, driving a skeletal aluminium go-kart around Ken Fox's wall of death to within six inches of the safety wire at the top—the wire that's there to prevent the machines sailing off into the crowd. "It's much more fun than helping kids on horses," she says, giggling nervously and brushing a strand of blonde hair back behind her ear. "The only thing I really miss about home is flush toilets."

6   Ken Fox and his wife Julie, their sons, Luke and Alex, and their troupe of Kerri, a new girl rider called Emma Starr, a man who prefers to be known just as Philip, and a wall-of-death enthusiast of an accountant named Neil Calladine, now operate the last wall of death in business in Britain. Calladine is the wall's "spieler", stalking the front of the attraction with a microphone, promising thrills and excitement as Ken and Luke Fox sit on their bikes, creating the roaring throttle noises of impending danger. Later, Luke and his father dip and zig-zag their bikes across each other, spinning round the drum every four seconds, as the holiday crowds peer tentatively down over the safety wire and then, in the traditional way, shower coins into the ring after being told that wall-of-death riders can never get insurance. Each show lasts 20 minutes; at one stage four riders are zipping up, down and all around.

7   In the 1930s and 1940s there were almost 30 walls of death at seaside resorts and fairgrounds around the country, often competing side-by-side in fairgrounds; now there are four left. One is in a steam museum in Derbyshire, another is the hobby/toy of a Cornish builder, and a third is owned by a 54-year-old agricultural engineer who "has done everything in motorcycles except ridden a wall of death". That wall's old owner, Graham Cripsey, of the Cripsey fairground family, is coming down from Skegness to teach him how to ride it.

8   Only Ken Fox and his band, together with pet dog Freebie, two ferrets and two cockatiels, tour in the traditional way, squelching out of their winter quarters from behind the Cambridgeshire hedgerows just before Easter and heading in convoy for the first of the 6,000 miles they will complete by the end of October. Ken is lucky that Julie can drive one of the trucks, change the 2 ft-high tyres, make sure Alex does his school lessons on his laptop, cook, make sandwiches and dish out the £2 tickets. She, too, loves the travelling life. "When you think I used to be a dental nurse," she says, her eyes misting a little.

9   She also helped her husband build his wall of death. "My old wall was wearing out," he says, "so I bought a 200 ft section of very long,

Page

very straight, Oregon pine that cost £70,000 (Oregon pine, one of the tallest trees in the world, is used for all walls of death because of the straightness of its grain and the lack of knot in its timber). I got the planks cut in a milling yard. I went to a boatyard where they built submarines. The place was so big we could have built 50 walls of death."

10   The motorbikes used for shows are Indian Scouts made in the 1920s by the Hendee Motorcycle Company of Springfield, Massachusetts, deliberately engineered for easy balance with all the controls on the left, so Chicago cops could use their right hands for drawing their revolvers and shooting at Al Capone-style gangsters. This means the bikes are perfect for tricks. Take your hand off the throttle of a modern motorbike and its slips back to idling mode, thus losing the power that keeps the bike on the wall. Take your hand off the throttle of an Indian Scout, and the revs stay as they are—which means that you can zoom round and round the wall of death, arms in the air, to your heart's content.

11   The first wall of death is said by Graham Cripsey to have come to Britain from America in 1928 with others close on its heels. His grandfather, Walter, and father, Roy, trained lions to ride in the sidecars, as did the famous George "Tornado" Smith at Southend's Kursaal fairground. The Cripseys also developed a technique of being towed round behind the Indian Scouts on roller skates. "If you were competing side by side in a fairground, you always had to have one stunt better than the other," explains Graham. Smith also kept a skeleton in a sidecar which, with a flick on a control, would suddenly sit bolt upright. And Ricky Abrey, 61, who rode with him as "The Black Baron", says Tornado perfected a ride where three riders would cut off their engines at the top of the wall and instantly re-start them again, causing the audience to gasp as 2 ft-long flashes of flame escaped the exhaust pipes.

12   Fun, then, for all the family. "People still love the wall of death," says Ken Fox emphatically. "People like what we put on and get good value for it. If they see it once, they always want to see it again. The problem is finding the people to work on it. There are a lot of soft men around."

13   "Wall of death" is, thankfully, a bit of a misnomer, for there have been no fatal accidents on British walls, though whether that's due to good luck or fear-induced careful preparation is difficult to tell. "I've been

knocked off by other riders, the engine's stalled, I've had punctures and I've hit a safety cable," says Ken Fox, pointing at his scars. "Everyone gets falls at some time but we try to be spot-on in our preparations. Before every show we spend a complete day trying to get the machines working perfectly."

14   Luke Fox suffered his first bad fall last year, flicking a safety-cable bolt on one of his "dips" as he zig-zagged his bike up and down. He fell 20 ft, got up and started again, even though he'd severely torn his knee. In a sense, he's got his own good-luck charm. His Indian bike was originally ridden by no less a daredevil than Tornado Smith himself. Luke has also inherited his father's total dedication to the trade and the Fox family wall looks set to last into the immediate future. Indeed, he and Kerri are now a partnership, sharing the long-haul driving and other things, while young Alex, the ferret-fancier, is raring for his first go at the wall.

15   Even Neil Calladine, the spieler, has shed his accountant duties and can indulge his lifelong passion for fairgrounds, though he needs to talk almost non-stop from 2 pm to 10 pm each show day and consumes mountains of throat sweets. "I make sure I go back and see the missus once a month," he says, "and of course I'm there all winter. I suppose I'm one of those fortunate people whose hobby has become his life. I love the freedom of travel, no nine-to-five, just us and the open road."

16   In that he's just like Kerri Cameron, bless her daredevil heart.

Adapted from an article
by John Dodd

[END OF PASSAGE]

[BLANK PAGE]

FOR OFFICIAL USE

G

Total
Mark

0860/404

NATIONAL
QUALIFICATIONS
2007

TUESDAY, 1 MAY
1.00 PM – 1.50 PM

ENGLISH
STANDARD GRADE
General Level
Reading
Questions

Fill in these boxes and read what is printed below.

Full name of centre

Town

Forename(s)

Surname

Date of birth
  Day Month Year   Scottish candidate number   Number of seat

**NB Before leaving the examination room you must give this booklet to the invigilator.
If you do not, you may lose all the marks for this paper.**

SCOTTISH
QUALIFICATIONS
AUTHORITY

©

Marks

QUESTIONS

Write your answers in the spaces provided.

Look at Paragraphs 1 to 3.

1. **In your own words**, explain fully why Kerri Cameron was looking up job vacancies on the internet.

   She was sick of her normal day job.

   2 1 0

2. What is surprising about Kerri's reaction to what her mother tells her about the wall of death?

   The fact she got excited and intrigued

   2 1 0

3. Why do you think Ken Fox was not interested in Kerri's school qualifications?

   The job required no qualifications

   2 ■ 0

Look at Paragraphs 4 and 5.

4. How does the writer suggest Kerri's enthusiasm after her test on the bike:

   (a) by word choice?

   "Fantastic" "The best"

   2 ■ 0

   (b) by sentence structure?

   Short sentences

   2 ■ 0

5. **Using your own words as far as possible**, describe **two** aspects of Kerri's performance which could be described as dangerous.

   The fact that she is go-karting around a perpendicular wall. with no safety.

   2 1 0

PAGE
TOTAL

Marks

Look at Paragraph 6.

6. **In your own words**, explain the job of the "spieler".

    He to be the commentator warm up the crowd   2   1   0

7. ". . . shower coins into the ring . . ."

    Give **two** reasons why "shower" is an effective word to use in this context.

    It gives the effect of lots of coins falling onto the stage   2   1   0

8. Why do you think members of the audience are told that wall-of-death riders "can never get insurance"?

    To build excitement and induce humour   2   0

9. Explain fully what the expression "zipping up, down and all around" suggests about the riders' performance.

    It is evidence they do not just stay on one place   2   1   0

Look at Paragraphs 7 to 9.

10. How does the writer illustrate the decline in popularity of walls of death?

    By using a list of the ones left   2   1   0

[Turn over

PAGE
TOTAL

Marks

11. "Only Ken Fox and his band . . ." (Paragraph 8)

Write down **one** word from earlier in the passage which contains the same idea as "band".

2 ■ 0

12. Explain fully why you think the writer uses the word "squelching" in Paragraph 8.

_____

_____

2 1 0

13. Look again at the sentence which begins "Ken is lucky . . ." (Paragraph 8).

How does the structure of the **whole** sentence help to reinforce how busy Julie is between Easter and October?

_____

_____

2 1 0

14. Why is Oregon pine so suitable for walls of death?

_____

2 1 0

Look at Paragraph 10.

15. Using your own words as far as possible, explain why the Indian Scout bikes are "perfect for tricks."

_____

_____

2 1 0

PAGE TOTAL

Marks

16. **Identify two techniques** used by the writer which help to involve the reader in his description of the Indian Scout motorbikes. **Quote evidence** from the paragraph to support your answers.

Technique	Evidence

2 1 0

2 1 0

Look at Paragraphs 11 and 12.

17. Why might the nicknames "Tornado" and "The Black Baron" be suitable for wall-of-death riders?

Tornado

_____

The Black Baron

_____

2 1 0

[Turn over

PAGE
TOTAL

Marks

18. (*a*)   Write down **four** things the early wall-of-death riders included in their acts.

_____

_____

_____

_____   2 | 1 | 0

(*b*)   **In your own words**, give **two** reasons why such things were included in the acts.

_____

_____   2 | 1 | 0

Look at Paragraphs 13 to 16.

19.   ". . . is, thankfully, a bit of a misnomer, . . ." (Paragraph 13)

(*a*)   Tick (✓) the box beside the best definition of "misnomer".

old-fashioned attraction	
risky venture	
successful show	
wrongly applied name	

(*b*)   Write down evidence from the passage to support your answer to 19(*a*).

_____   2 | 1 | 0

20.   Why is the word "dips" (Paragraph 14) in inverted commas?

_____   2 | ■ | 0

PAGE TOTAL

Marks

21. Give **three** pieces of evidence to support the writer's statement that "the Fox family wall looks set to last into the immediate future" (Paragraph 14).

_____

_____

_____   2   1   0

22. Show how the final paragraph is an effective conclusion to this article.

_____

_____   2   1   0

[*END OF QUESTION PAPER*]

PAGE
TOTAL

FOR OFFICIAL USE

[0860/404]

p2 ☐

p3 ☐

p4 ☐

p5 ☐

p6 ☐

p7 ☐

TOTAL
MARK ☐

FOR OFFICIAL USE

[BLANK PAGE]

C

0860/405

NATIONAL
QUALIFICATIONS
2007

TUESDAY, 1 MAY
2.30 PM – 3.20 PM

ENGLISH
STANDARD GRADE
Credit Level
Reading
Text

Read carefully the passage overleaf. It will help if you read it twice. When you have done so, answer the questions. Use the spaces provided in the Question/Answer booklet.

SCOTTISH
QUALIFICATIONS
AUTHORITY

SA 0860/405 6/46170

©

DARKNESS AND LIGHT

In this passage Kathleen Jamie describes a visit to Maes Howe, one of the most important archaeological sites on Orkney. Her visit takes place in December, just before the winter solstice—the shortest day of the year.

1   The building nowadays known as Maes Howe is a Neolithic chambered cairn, a tomb where, 5000 years ago, they interred the bones of the dead. In its long, long existence it has been more forgotten about than known, but in our era it is open to the public, with tickets and guides and explanatory booklets. It stands, a mere grassy hump in a field, in the central plain of Mainland Orkney. There is a startling collection of other Neolithic sites nearby.

2   To reach Maes Howe I took the road that passes over a thin isthmus between two lochs. On the west side is a huge brooding stone circle, the Ring of Brodgar. On the east, like three elegant women conversing at a cocktail party, are the Standing Stones of Stenness. The purpose of these may be mysterious, but a short seven miles away is the Neolithic village called Skara Brae. There is preserved a huddle of roofless huts, dug half underground into midden and sand dune. There, you can marvel at the domestic normality, that late Stone Age people had beds and cupboards and neighbours and beads. You can feel both their presence, their day-to-day lives, and their utter absence. It's a good place to go. It re-calibrates your sense of time.

3   Two men were standing at the car park at Maes Howe. The taller, older man was wearing a white shirt and improbable tartan trousers. As I stepped out of the car, he shook his head sadly. The younger man was dressed for outdoors, somewhat like a traffic warden, with a woollen hat pulled down to his eyes and a navy-blue coat. For a moment we all looked at each other. The taller man spoke first.

4   "Not looking good, I'm afraid."

5   The timing was right, the sun was setting, but . . .

6   "Cloud," said the tall man.

7   "Can't be helped," I replied.

8   "Will you go in, anyway? You can't always tell, you just need a moment when the cloud breaks . . ."

9   Alan, an Englishman in Historic Scotland tartan trousers, led me into a little shop to issue a ticket. The shop was housed in an old water mill, some distance from the tomb, and sold guidebooks and fridge magnets and tea towels. From the window you could see over the main road to the tomb.

10   "Tell you what," he said. "I'll give you a ticket so you can come back tomorrow, if you like, but I can't give you one for the actual solstice, Saturday. We start selling them at two-thirty on the actual solstice. It's first come, first served."

11   "How many people come?"

12   "Well, we can accommodate 25, at a pinch."

13   But today there was only myself.

14   The young guide, Rob, was waiting outside. A workman's van hurtled past, then we crossed the road, entered through a wicket gate and followed a path across the field. We were walking toward the tomb by an indirect route that respected the wide ditch around the site. Sheep were grazing the field, and a heron was standing with its aristocratic back to us. There was a breeze, and the shivery call of a curlew descending. On all sides there are low hills, holding the plain between them. To the

south, the skyline is dominated by two much bigger, more distant hills, a peak and a plateau. Though you wouldn't know it from here, they belong to another island, to Hoy. Above these dark hills, in horizontal bars, were the offending clouds.

*   *   *

15   You enter into the inner chamber of the tomb by a low passageway more than 25 feet long. It's more of a journey than a gateway. You don't have to crawl on hands and knees, but neither can you walk upright. The stone roof bears down on your spine; a single enormous slab of stone forms the wall you brush with your left shoulder. You must walk in that stooped position just a moment too long, so when you're admitted to the cairn two sensations come at once: you're glad to stand, and the other is a sudden appreciation of stone. You are admitted into a solemn place.

16   You are standing in a high, dim stone vault. There is a thick soundlessness, like a recording studio, or a strongroom. A moment ago, you were in the middle of a field, with the wind and curlews calling. That world has been taken away, and the world you have entered into is not like a cave, but a place of artifice, of skill. Yes, that's it, what you notice when you stand and look around is cool, dry, applied skill. Across five thousand years you can still feel their self-assurance.

17   The walls are of red sandstone, dressed into long rectangles, with a tall sentry-like buttress in each corner to support the corbelled roof. The passage to the outside world is at the base of one wall. Set waist-high into the other three are square openings into cells which disappear into the thickness of the walls. That's where they laid the dead, once the bones had been cleaned of flesh by weather and birds. The stone blocks which would once have sealed these graves lie on the gravel floor. And the point is, the ancients who built this tomb lined it up precisely: the long passageway faces exactly the setting midwinter sun. Consequently, for the few days around the winter solstice a beam of the setting sun shines along the passage, and onto the tomb's back wall. In recent years, people have crept along the passageway at midwinter to witness this. Some, apparently, find it overwhelming.

*   *   *

18   We crossed the field. The heron took to the air. I dawdled behind. My guide, the young Rob, was waiting at the entrance, which is just a low square opening at the bottom of the mound. I glanced back at the outside world, the road, the clouded sky over Hoy's hills, which did not look promising; then we crept inside and for a long minute walked doubled over, until Rob stood and I followed.

19   Inside was bright as a tube train, and the effect was brutal. I'd expected not utter darkness, but perhaps a dullish red. Rob was carrying a torch but this light revealed every crack, every joint and fissure in the ancient stonework. At once a man's voice said, "Sorry, I'll switch it off," but the moment was lost and, anyway, I'd been forewarned. As he sold me the ticket, Alan had told me that surveyors were inside the cairn, with all their equipment. "A bit of a problem", was how he'd put it. And here they were. We entered the tomb and, in that fierce white light, it was like that moment which can occur in midlife, when you look at your mother and realise with a shock that she is old.

20   The surveyors were doing a project that involved laser-scanning, photogrammetry, and pulse-radar inspection. They were working inside the tomb, and had been for days. A huge implement, I couldn't tell if it was a torch or a camera, lay on a schoolroom chair. There was a telephone in one of the grave-cells. There were two surveyors. One was folded, foetus-like, into the little cell in the back wall. I could see only his legs. He grunted as he shifted position.

21   "Strange place to spend your working day," I remarked.

22   "You're not wrong," he replied, sourly.

23   His older colleague seemed glad for a break. He stood, a portly man in a black tracksuit and fleece jacket, and stretched his back. Somehow he dimmed the light and the tomb settled back into restful gloom. The outside world was a square at the far end of the long passageway. There would be no sunset.

24   "Too bad," the surveyor said. "Oh, well."

25   Rob, hunched in his woolly hat, drew breath and raised his torch as though to begin the guided tour, but he paused.

26   "Been here before?" he asked me.

27   "Several times."

28   He said, "We're on the Web now, y'know," and gestured with the torch to a camera mounted on the Neolithic wall. "Live. Don't go picking your nose."

29   "Watch your eyes!" said the voice from the grave-chamber, then came a detonating flash.

[END OF PASSAGE]

FOR OFFICIAL USE

C

Total
Mark

0860/406

NATIONAL
QUALIFICATIONS
2007

TUESDAY, 1 MAY
2.30 PM – 3.20 PM

ENGLISH
STANDARD GRADE
Credit Level
Reading
Questions

Fill in these boxes and read what is printed below.

Full name of centre

Town

Forename(s)

Surname

Date of birth
Day Month Year   Scottish candidate number   Number of seat

**NB Before leaving the examination room you must give this booklet to the invigilator.
If you do not, you may lose all the marks for this paper.**

SCOTTISH
QUALIFICATIONS
AUTHORITY

QUESTIONS

Write your answers in the spaces provided.

Look at Paragraphs 1 and 2.

1. Give the meaning of "interred" and show how the context helped you to arrive at that meaning.

    Meaning: _____

    Context: _____　　2 1

2. Write down **two** examples of the writer's use of **contrast** from Paragraph 1.

    _____

    _____　　2 1

3. "a thin isthmus" (Paragraph 2)

    Tick the box beside the best definition of "isthmus".

area of land	
strip of land with water on each side	
stretch of moorland	
bridge connecting two islands	

    2 ■

4. Identify the figure of speech used by the writer to describe the Standing Stones of Stenness. What does it suggest about the stones?

    _____

    _____　　2 1

5. **In your own words**, explain what the writer finds to "marvel at" in the village of Skara Brae.

    _____

    _____　　2 1

Marks

6. What do you think the writer means when she says Skara Brae "re-calibrates your sense of time"?

_____

_____   2 1 0

Look at Paragraphs 3 to 8.

7. Why do you think the writer uses "improbable" to describe the older man's tartan trousers?

_____   2 ■ 0

8. Why does the man shake his head sadly as the writer steps out of her car?

_____   2 ■ 0

Look at Paragraphs 9 to 14.

9. Give **three** pieces of evidence which suggest that Maes Howe is just like any other tourist attraction.

_____

_____

_____   2 1 0

10. In your own words, give **two** reasons why the writer cannot buy a ticket in advance for the solstice.

_____

_____   2 1 0

[Turn over

PAGE
TOTAL

Marks

11. Comment on the writer's use of word choice **and** sentence structure in her description of the clouds in the final sentence of Paragraph 14.

(*a*)   Word choice:

_____

_____   2   1

(*b*)   Sentence structure:

_____

_____   2   1

Look at Paragraphs 15 and 16.

12. In what way is entry to the inner chamber "more of a journey than a gateway"?

_____   2   ■

13. In your own words, describe **two** sensations which might be felt by someone entering the cairn.

_____

_____   2   1

14. What does a visitor notice and feel about the builders of Maes Howe? **Answer in your own words**.

_____

_____   2   1

15. (*a*)   What style does the writer adopt in Paragraphs 15 and 16?

_____   2   ■

(*b*)   Support your answer with **two** pieces of evidence.

_____   2   1

PAGE
TOTAL

Marks

Look at Paragraph 17.

16. Why did the builders of Maes Howe position it as they did?

_____

_____   2 | 1 | 0

17. What does the use of the word "apparently" tell you about the writer's attitude to the idea that some people find the experience in the tomb "overwhelming"?

_____   2 | ■ | 0

Look at Paragraphs 18 and 19.

18. Why was the inside of the tomb "as bright as a tube train"?

_____   2 | 1 | 0

19. Why do you think the writer includes the **comparison** of looking at her mother at the end of Paragraph 19?

_____

_____   2 | 1 | 0

[Turn over for Questions 20 to 23 on *Page six*

PAGE
TOTAL

Marks

Look at Paragraphs 20 to 28.

20. What evidence is there that the surveyors are doing a **thorough** job inside Maes Howe?

_____

_____   2 1

21. Give a possible reason for the surveyor answering the writer "sourly".

_____   2 ■

22. In what way has Maes Howe become more accessible?

_____   2 1

Think about the passage as a whole.

23. Why might "Darkness and Light" be considered an appropriate title for this passage?

_____

_____   2 1

[END OF QUESTION PAPER]

PAGE
TOTAL

STANDARD GRADE | GENERAL

2008
READING

[BLANK PAGE]

G

0860/403

NATIONAL
QUALIFICATIONS
2008

TUESDAY, 6 MAY
1.00 PM – 1.50 PM

ENGLISH
STANDARD GRADE
General Level
Reading
Text

Read carefully the passage overleaf. It will help if you read it twice. When you have done so, answer the questions. Use the spaces provided in the Question/Answer booklet.

SQA
©

Saddle the white horses

Thurso prepares to host its first professional surf tour, confirming Scotland's status as a world–class surfing destination.

1   It was the stickers that gave it away. Turning left on the A9 at Latheron in Caithness, you were suddenly faced with a sign that looked as though it had been defaced by advertising executives from surfing companies. Like a cairn on a mountain path, the big green board declaring Thurso to be 23 miles away told travelling bands of surfers that they'd taken the right turn-off and were nearly at their destination. Slapping another sticker on the sign was like laying another stone on the pile.

2   Thurso is about to enter surfing's big league.

3   It's hard to reconcile the popular tropical imagery of surfing with the town, a raw, exposed kind of place that enjoys little escape from the worst excesses of the Scottish climate. The Caithness coastline is peppered with surfing spots, but the jewel in the crown and the target for dedicated wave riders lies within spitting distance of Thurso town centre at a reef break called Thurso East. In the right conditions, the swell there rears up over kelp-covered slabs into a fast-moving, barrelling monster of a wave considered world class by those in the know.

4   Now Thurso East is the focus of a huge professional surfing tour. The week-long Highland Open marks the first time a World Qualifying Series (WQS) surfing competition has been held in Scotland. It will also be the furthest north a WQS tour has ever travelled, anywhere in the world.

5   Professional competitive surfing has two tours: the WQS and the World Championship Tour (WCT). The WCT is the premier division, with the WQS being used as a platform for professionals to move up into the big time. Around 160 up-and-coming wave riders are expected to take part in the Thurso event. Prize money of $100,000 (£57,000) is up for grabs, along with vital tour points.

6   "Travelling and exploring new places is part of the whole surfing culture," says Bernhard Ritzer, the Highland Open event manager. "We've had so much feedback from surfers from Australia and Brazil who want to go. They see it as an adventure and as something new. We did a photo trip there last year with some of our team riders and they were impressed. They're excited about it—although it will still be a shock because I don't think they know how cold and harsh it can be."

7   "Thurso is one of the best waves in Europe, if not the world," he says. "Most people don't even know it, and it's just so good. It doesn't always have to be sunny, warm and tropical. It can also be cold, rough and hard.

8   "The idea is to have a contrast to the summer events in the tropical islands. We also have something in the north to show that this is part of surfing. Very often on the WQS tour the waves aren't that good, but here they are expecting big reef break waves and they like to surf those."

9   Surfers generally guard their local breaks jealously. It's considered essential to keep your mouth shut about your "secret spot", in case you find it overrun with visitors. So, economic benefits to Thurso aside, some local surfers were a little concerned about an event on this scale descending on their area. WQS representatives met with these surfers to address their concerns and feel that they've pretty much got everyone on board. WQS is also paying for improvements to the car parking area near the Thurso East break.

10   "We're concerned to get the locals involved," says Ritzer. "We want to keep them happy and don't want to look too commercial, coming in with a big event machine. We need them to help organise local stuff. You always have some individuals who will boycott everything, but we understand that most of them are positive."

11   Andy Bain probably knows the break at Thurso East better than anyone, although he'll be watching the competition from the shoreline. Bain, who runs Thurso Surf, has been surfing the reef there for 17 years and is eagerly anticipating the arrival of the Highland Open. He's aware of the concerns and the possible exposure of his home break, but doesn't anticipate a negative impact.

12   "From the surf school side of things it's good because it'll generate business for us," says Bain, 33. "As a local surfer, it's kind of like closure for me to have this competition. To say the world has now recognised Thurso as a top surfing destination makes me feel proud. A lot of people say it's going to get crowded and exposed, but with it being a cold destination I don't think it's going to be that bad."

13   For professional surfer Adam Robertson from Victoria, Australia, the trip to Thurso will be something of a journey into the unknown. "This will be the first time I've ever been to Scotland," says Robertson, who has competed on the WQS tour for the past three years. "We're all a bit worried about how cold it's going to be. Apart from that we're pretty excited because it's a place we've never been."

14   Robertson, 23, who has been surfing since he was four, criss-crosses the globe with his fellow WQS competitors in pursuit of the best waves and a place on the coveted WCT tour. He may as well be going to surf on the moon for all he knows about Thurso East, but that's part of the appeal.

15   "We follow the surf around all year and go to a lot of different places, but Scotland's somewhere probably none of us have been to," he says. "That for me was a big part of wanting to go, to see the place. As a professional surfer, you've got to live out of your bag a lot, travelling around with long stints away from home, but when you perform well in the event or get some really good waves, it makes it all worth it.

16   "I feel pretty good and I'm hoping to do well," he adds. "Everyone who does the tour is feeling good too, so it should be a great event. It'll be interesting to see what the waves are like."

17   Competitors will be scored by a team of eight international judges on the length of their ride, the difficulty of moves and how they connect it all together. Waves are scored on a one to ten scale, with ten a perfect ride, and the final scores are based on each surfer's two highest-scoring waves.

18   "These events raise the profile of locations, create investment in areas and hopefully provide opportunities for young surfers coming through to grow and compete at world-class levels," says Dave Reed, contest director for the WQS event. "It's a great way to say we've got some of the best waves in the world."

Adapted from a magazine article

[END OF PASSAGE]

[BLANK PAGE]

FOR OFFICIAL USE

G

Total Mark

0860/404

NATIONAL
QUALIFICATIONS
2008

TUESDAY, 6 MAY
1.00 PM – 1.50 PM

**ENGLISH
STANDARD GRADE**
General Level
Reading
Questions

Fill in these boxes and read what is printed below.

Full name of centre

Town

Forename(s)

Surname

Date of birth
　Day　Month　Year

Scottish candidate number

Number of seat

**NB Before leaving the examination room you must give this booklet to the invigilator.
If you do not, you may lose all the marks for this paper.**

SA 0860/404 6/66870

Marks

QUESTIONS

Write your answers in the spaces provided.

Look at Paragraphs 1 to 3.

1. (*a*) What had been added to the road sign in Caithness?

   _____   2 ■ 0

   (*b*) Write down **two** things the surfers would know when they saw this road sign.

   _____

   _____   2 1 0

2. "Thurso is about to enter surfing's big league." (Paragraph 2)

   How does the writer make this statement stand out?

   _____   2 ■ 0

3. Thurso is different from the popular image of a surfing location.

   (*a*) **In your own words**, describe the popular image of a surfing location.

   _____   2 ■ 0

   (*b*) **Write down an expression** showing how Thurso is different.

   _____   2 ■ 0

4. What do the words "jewel in the crown" (Paragraph 3) suggest about Thurso East?

   _____   2 ■ 0

5. ". . . a fast-moving, barrelling monster . . ." (Paragraph 3)

   Explain fully why this is an effective description of the wave.

   _____

   _____   2 1

PAGE
TOTAL

Marks

Look at Paragraphs 4 and 5.

6. In which **two** ways is the Highland Open different from other WQS surfing competitions?

(i) _____

(ii) _____   2   1   0

7. In your own words, explain the difference between the two professional surfing tours.

WCT _____

WQS _____   2   1   0

8. Which **two** benefits will the winner of the competition gain?

(i) _____

(ii) _____   2   1   0

Look at Paragraphs 6 to 8.

9. Give **three** reasons why, according to Bernhard Ritzer, surfers will want to visit Thurso.

(i) _____

(ii) _____

(iii) _____   2   1   0

10. According to Ritzer, what will surprise the surfers?

_____   2   ■   0

[Turn over

PAGE
TOTAL

Marks

11. Thurso can offer something which many other surfing locations cannot.

What is this?

_____

2 ■ 0

Look at Paragraphs 9 and 10.

12. "Surfers generally guard their local breaks . . . " (Paragraph 9)

In your own words, explain why surfers do this.

_____

2 1 0

13. What **style** of language is used in the expression "keep your mouth shut" (Paragraph 9)?

_____

2 ■ 0

14. Which **two key** things have WQS representatives done to gain support?

(i) _____

(ii) _____

2 1 0

15. The WQS representatives feel that "they've pretty much got everyone on board." (Paragraph 9)

Write down an expression from Paragraph 10 which continues this idea.

_____

2 ■ 0

16. **Write down a single word** from this section meaning "refuse to support or take part".

2 ■ 0

PAGE
TOTAL

Marks

Look at Paragraphs 11 to 18.

17. (*a*)   How does local surfer Andy Bain feel about the competition?

Tick (✓) the best answer.

very negative and angry	
quite pleased but worried	
excited and not really anxious	

2 ■ 0

(*b*)   **Write down an expression** to support your chosen answer.

_____

2 ■ 0

18.   "He may as well be going to surf on the moon . . . "   (Paragraph 14)

What does this comparison suggest about Thurso?

_____

2 ■ 0

19.   In Paragraph 15, Australian Adam Robertson describes his life as a professional surfer.

In your own words, sum up the **negative** and **positive** aspects of his life.

(*a*)   **negative:** _____

_____

2 1 0

(*b*)   **positive:** _____

_____

2 1 0

20.   What **three** elements of the surfers' performance are judged?

(i) _____

(ii) _____

(iii) _____

2 1 0

[Turn over

PAGE
TOTAL

Marks

Think about the passage as a whole.

21. (i) What do you think is the main purpose of this passage?

Tick (✓) **one** box.

to tell the reader some amusing stories about surfing	
to inform the reader about a surfing competition in Scotland	
to argue against holding a surfing competition in Scotland	

(ii) Give a reason to support your answer.

_____

_____

2 1 0

[END OF QUESTION PAPER]

PAGE
TOTAL

FOR OFFICIAL USE

[0860/404]

p2	
p3	
p4	
p5	
p6	
TOTAL MARK	

FOR OFFICIAL USE

[BLANK PAGE]

[BLANK PAGE]

C

0860/405

| NATIONAL QUALIFICATIONS 2008 | TUESDAY, 6 MAY 2.30 PM – 3.20 PM | ENGLISH STANDARD GRADE Credit Level Reading Text |

Read carefully the passage overleaf. It will help if you read it twice. When you have done so, answer the questions. Use the spaces provided in the Question/Answer booklet.

This passage, taken from the opening chapter of a novel, introduces us to the character of Briony and her family.

1   The play—for which Briony had designed the posters, programmes and tickets, constructed the sales booth out of a folding screen tipped on its side, and lined the collection box in red crêpe paper—was written by her in a two-day tempest of composition, causing her to miss a breakfast and a lunch. When the preparations were complete, she had nothing to do but contemplate her finished draft and wait for the appearance of her cousins from the distant north. There would be time for only one day of rehearsal before her brother, Leon, arrived.

2   At some moments chilling, at others desperately sad, the play told a tale of the heart whose message, conveyed in a rhyming prologue, was that love which did not build a foundation on good sense was doomed. The reckless passion of the heroine, Arabella, for a wicked foreign count is punished by ill fortune when she contracts cholera during an impetuous dash towards a seaside town with her intended. Deserted by him and nearly everybody else, bed-bound in an attic, she discovers in herself a sense of humour. Fortune presents her a second chance in the form of an impoverished doctor—in fact, a prince in disguise who has elected to work among the needy. Healed by him, Arabella chooses wisely this time, and is rewarded by reconciliation with her family and a wedding with the medical prince on "a windy sunlit day in spring".

3   Mrs Tallis read the seven pages of *The Trials of Arabella* in her bedroom, at her dressing table, with the author's arm around her shoulder the whole while. Briony studied her mother's face for every trace of shifting emotion, and Emily Tallis obliged with looks of alarm, snickers of glee and, at the end, grateful smiles and wise, affirming nods. She took her daughter in her arms, onto her lap, and said that the play was "stupendous", and agreed instantly, murmuring into the girl's ear, that this word could be quoted on the poster which was to be on an easel in the entrance hall by the ticket booth.

4   Briony was hardly to know it then, but this was the project's highest point of fulfilment. Nothing came near it for satisfaction, all else was dreams and frustration. There were moments in the summer dusk after her light was out, burrowing in the delicious gloom of her canopy bed, when she made her heart thud with luminous, yearning fantasies, little playlets in themselves, every one of which featured Leon. In one, his big, good-natured face buckled in grief as Arabella sank in loneliness and despair. In another, there he was, cocktail in hand at some fashionable city bar, overheard boasting to a group of friends: Yes, my younger sister, Briony Tallis the writer, you must surely have heard of her. In a third he punched the air in exultation as the final curtain fell, although there was no curtain, there was no possibility of a curtain. Her play was not for her cousins, it was for her brother, to celebrate his return, provoke his admiration and guide him away from his careless succession of girlfriends, towards the right form of wife, the one who would persuade him to return to the countryside, the one who would sweetly request Briony's services as a bridesmaid.

5   She was one of those children possessed by a desire to have the world just so. Whereas her big sister's room was a stew of unclosed books, unfolded clothes, unmade bed, unemptied ashtrays, Briony's was a shrine to her controlling demon: the model farm spread across a deep window ledge consisted of the usual animals, but all facing one way—towards their owner—as if about to break into song, and even the farmyard hens were neatly corralled. In fact, Briony's was the only tidy upstairs

room in the house. Her straight-backed dolls in their many-roomed mansion appeared to be under strict instructions not to touch the walls; the various thumb-sized figures to be found standing about her dressing table—cowboys, deep-sea divers, humanoid mice—suggested by their even ranks and spacing a citizen army awaiting orders.

6   A taste for the miniature was one aspect of an orderly spirit. Another was a passion for secrets: in a prized varnished cabinet, a secret drawer was opened by pushing against the grain of a cleverly turned dovetail joint, and here she kept a diary locked by a clasp, and a notebook written in a code of her own invention. In a toy safe opened by six secret numbers she stored letters and postcards. An old tin petty cash box was hidden under a removable floorboard beneath her bed. In the box were treasures that dated back four years, to her ninth birthday when she began collecting: a mutant double acorn, fool's gold, a rain-making spell bought at a funfair, a squirrel's skull as light as a leaf.

7   At the age of eleven she wrote her first story—a foolish affair, imitative of half a dozen folk tales and lacking, she realised later, that vital knowingness about the ways of the world which compels a reader's respect. But this first clumsy attempt showed her that the imagination itself was a source of secrets: once she had begun a story, no one could be told. Pretending in words was too tentative, too vulnerable, too embarrassing to let anyone know. Even writing out the *she saids*, the *and thens*, made her wince, and she felt foolish, appearing to know about the emotions of an imaginary being. Self-exposure was inevitable the moment she described a character's weakness; the reader was bound to speculate that she was describing herself. What other authority could she have? Only when a story was finished could she feel immune, and ready to punch holes in the margins, bind the chapters with pieces of string, paint or draw the cover, and take the finished work to show to her mother, or her father, when he was home.

8   Her efforts received encouragement. In fact, they were welcomed as the Tallises began to understand that the baby of the family possessed a strange mind and a facility with words. Briony was encouraged to read her stories aloud in the library and it surprised her parents and older sister to hear their quiet girl perform so boldly, making big gestures with her free arm, arching her eyebrows as she did the voices, and looking up from the page for seconds at a time as she read in order to gaze into one face after the other, unapologetically demanding her family's total attention as she cast her narrative spell.

9   The play she had written for Leon's homecoming was her first attempt at drama, and she had found the change quite effortless. It was a relief not to be writing out the *she saids*, or describing the weather or the onset of spring or her heroine's face—beauty, she had discovered, occupied a narrow band. Ugliness, on the other hand, had infinite variation. *The Trials of Arabella* was intended to inspire not laughter, but terror, relief and instruction, in that order, and the innocent intensity with which Briony set about the project—the posters, tickets, sales booth—made her particularly vulnerable to failure.

[END OF PASSAGE]

[BLANK PAGE]

FOR OFFICIAL USE

C

Total Mark

0860/406

NATIONAL
QUALIFICATIONS
2008

TUESDAY, 6 MAY
2.30 PM – 3.20 PM

**ENGLISH
STANDARD GRADE**
Credit Level
Reading
Questions

Fill in these boxes and read what is printed below.

Full name of centre

Town

Forename(s)

Surname

Date of birth
Day   Month   Year

Scottish candidate number

Number of seat

NB Before leaving the examination room you must give this booklet to the invigilator. If you do not, you may lose all the marks for this paper.

Marks

QUESTIONS

Write your answers in the spaces provided.

Look at Paragraph 1.

1. What task has Briony been involved in?

   _____   2 ■ 0

2. In Paragraph 1, the writer shows how committed Briony has been to this task.

   Explain how **sentence structure** and **word choice** indicate Briony's high level of commitment.

   (*a*)   **sentence structure:**

   _____

   _____   2 1 0

   (*b*)   **word choice:**

   _____

   _____   2 1 0

Look at Paragraph 2.

3. Briony's play is a story with a message.

   In your own words, explain what the message is.

   _____

   _____   2 1 0

PAGE
TOTAL

Marks

4. Read the writer's description of Briony's play in Paragraph 2, beginning: "The reckless passion of the heroine . . ."

   (*a*) What seems to be the writer's attitude to Briony's play?

   _____

   2　1　0

   (*b*) Quote **one** detail from the description and explain how it conveys this attitude.

   _____

   _____

   _____

   2　1　0

Look at Paragraph 3.

5. ". . . and Emily Tallis obliged . . ." (Paragraph 3)

   What does the word "**obliged**" suggest about Emily's reaction to the play?

   _____

   2　■　0

6. Give **two** ways in which the writer emphasises the closeness between Briony and her mother.

   (i) _____

   (ii) _____

   2　1　0

Look at Paragraphs 4 and 5.

7. We are told that Briony's imagination took over "after her light was out". (Paragraph 4)

   By **referring closely** to the passage, **explain** how the writer's word choice indicates the **intensity** of Briony's fantasies.

   _____

   _____

   2　1　0

[Turn over

PAGE
TOTAL

Marks

8. How does Briony want her brother, Leon, to **feel** about her writing?

Quote an expression from the passage to support your answer.

_____

_____   **2 1 0**

9. Look closely at the **final sentence** of Paragraph 4.

In your own words, give **two** reasons why Briony has written the play for her brother.

_____

_____   **2 1 0**

10. In Paragraph 5, the writer develops a **contrast** between Briony and her big sister.

(*a*) **In your own words**, state what the contrast is.

_____

_____   **2 1 0**

(*b*) By referring to **sentence structure** and **word choice**, explain how this contrast is developed.

You should refer to **both** characters in **both** parts of your answer.

(i) **sentence structure:** _____

_____

_____

_____   **2 1 0**

(ii) **word choice:** _____

_____

_____

_____   **2 1 0**

PAGE TOTAL

Marks

11. Explain the function of the **dashes** in the expression "— towards their owner—". (Paragraph 5)

_____

2 | 1 | 0

Look at Paragraph 6.

12. "Another was a passion for secrets:" (Paragraph 6)

By referring to the passage, show how the writer continues this idea in the rest of the paragraph.

_____

_____

2 | 1 | 0

13. Explain why a **colon** is used in the expression "when she began collecting:" (Paragraph 6)

_____

2 | 1 | 0

14. What do the items in Briony's collection suggest about her as a person?

_____

2 | ■ | 0

Look at Paragraph 7.

15. Briony wrote her first story when she was eleven.

In your own words, give **two** reasons why she later disliked this story.

(i) _____

(ii) _____

2 | 1 | 0

16. Explain **in your own words** why Briony was concerned about describing a character's weakness.

_____

_____

2 | 1 | 0

[Turn over for Questions 17 to 20 on *Page six*

PAGE TOTAL

Marks

17. **Quote one** word from Paragraph 7 showing that Briony was no longer vulnerable when the story was finished.

2

Look at Paragraphs 8 and 9.

18. Explain why Briony's performance in the library surprised her family.

    Answer in your own words.

    _____

    _____

2

19. Why did Briony prefer writing about **ugly** rather than **beautiful** characters?

    Use your own words in your explanation.

    _____

    _____

2

Think about the passage as a whole.

20. In Briony, the writer has created a character who is both **imaginative** and **anxious**.

    By referring closely to the passage, show how both these aspects of her personality have been conveyed to the reader.

    (i) **imaginative:**

    _____

    _____

2

    (ii) **anxious:**

    _____

    _____

2

[END OF QUESTION PAPER]

STANDARD GRADE | GENERAL

2009
READING

[BLANK PAGE]

G

0860/403

NATIONAL
QUALIFICATIONS
2009

FRIDAY, 8 MAY
1.00 PM – 1.50 PM

ENGLISH
STANDARD GRADE
General Level
Reading
Text

Read carefully the passage overleaf. It will help if you read it twice. When you have done so, answer the questions. Use the spaces provided in the Question/Answer booklet.

In the following passage, Alice, the main character, is spending the summer working in France.

1   Alice notices a fly on the underside of her arm.

2   Insects are an occupational hazard at a dig, and for some reason there are more flies higher up the mountain where she is working than at the main excavation site lower down.

3   Her concentration broken, Alice stands up and stretches. She unscrews the top of her water bottle. It's warm, but she's too thirsty to care and drinks it down in great gulps. Below, the heat haze shimmers above the dented tarmac of the road. Above her, the sky is an endless blue.

4   It's her first time in the Pyrenees, although she feels very much at home. In the main camp on the lower slopes, Alice can see her colleagues standing under the big canvas awning. She's surprised they've stopped already. It's early in the day to be taking a break, but then the whole team is a bit demoralised. It's hard work: the digging, scraping, cataloguing, recording, and so far they've turned up little to justify their efforts. They've come across only a few fragments of early medieval pots and bowls, and a couple of arrowheads.

5   Alice is tempted to go down and join her colleagues. Her calves are already aching from squatting. The muscles in her shoulders are tense. But she knows that if she stops now, she'll lose her momentum.

6   Hopefully, her luck's about to change. Earlier, she'd noticed something glinting beneath a large boulder, propped against the side of the mountain, almost as if it had been placed there by a giant hand. Although she can't make out what the object is, even how big it is, she's been digging all morning and she doesn't think it will be much longer before she can reach it.

7   She knows she should fetch someone. Alice is not a trained archaeologist, just a volunteer. But it's her last day on site and she wants to prove herself. If she goes back down to the main camp now and admits she's on to something, everybody will want to be involved, and it will no longer be her discovery.

8   In the days and weeks to come, Alice will look back to this moment. She will wonder at how different things might have been had she made the choice to go and not to stay. If she had played by the rules.

9   She drains the last drop of water from the bottle and tosses it into her rucksack. For the next hour or so, as the sun climbs higher in the sky and the temperature rises, Alice carries on working. The only sounds are the scrape of metal on rock, the whine of insects and the occasional buzz of a light aircraft in the distance.

10   Alice kneels down on the ground and leans her cheek and shoulder against the rock for support. Then, with a flutter of excitement, she pushes her fingers deep into the dark earth. Straight away, she knows she's got something worth finding. It is smooth to the touch, metal not stone. Grasping it firmly and telling herself not to expect too much, slowly, slowly she eases the object out into the light.

11   The rich, cloying smell of wet soil fills her nose and throat, although she barely notices. She is already lost in the past, captivated by the piece of history she cradles in the palms of her hands. It is a heavy, round buckle, speckled black and green with age and from its long burial.

12   Alice is so absorbed that she doesn't notice the boulder shifting on its base. Then something makes her look up. For a split second, the world seems to hang suspended, out of space, out of time. She is mesmerised by the ancient slab of stone as it sways and tilts, and then gracefully begins to fall towards her. At the very last moment, the light fractures. The spell is broken. Alice throws herself out of the way, half tumbling, half slithering sideways, just in time to avoid being crushed. The boulder hits the ground with a dull thud, sending up a cloud of pale brown dust, then rolls over and over, as if in slow motion, until it comes to rest further down the mountain.

13   Alice clutches desperately at the bushes and scrub to stop herself slipping any further. For a moment she lies sprawled in the dirt, dizzy and disorientated. As it sinks in how very close she came to being crushed, she turns cold. Takes a deep breath. Waits for the world to stop spinning.

14   Gradually, the pounding in her head dies away. The sickness in her stomach settles and everything starts to return to normal, enough for her to sit up and take stock. Her knees are grazed and streaked with blood and she's knocked her wrist where she landed awkwardly, still clutching the buckle in her hand to protect it, but basically she's escaped with no more than a few cuts and bruises.

15   She gets to her feet and dusts herself down. She raises her hand, is about to call out to attract someone's attention when she notices that there's a narrow opening visible in the side of the mountain where the boulder had been standing. Like a doorway cut into the rock.

16   She hesitates. Alice knows she should get somebody to come with her. It is stupid, possibly even dangerous, to go in on her own without any sort of back-up. She knows all the things that can go wrong. But something is drawing her in. It feels personal. It's her discovery.

17   She climbs back up. There is a dip in the ground at the mouth of the cave, where the stone had stood guard. The damp earth is alive with the frantic writhing of worms and beetles exposed suddenly to the light and heat after so long. Her cap lies on the ground where it fell. Her trowel is there too, just where she left it.

18   Alice peers into the darkness. The opening is no more than five feet high and about three feet wide and the edges are irregular and rough. It seems to be natural rather than man-made.

19   Slowly, her eyes become accustomed to the gloom. Velvet black gives way to charcoal grey and she sees that she is looking into a long, narrow tunnel.

20   Squeezing the buckle tightly in her hand, she takes a deep breath and steps forward into the passageway. Straight away, the smell of long-hidden, underground air surrounds her, filling her mouth and throat and lungs. It's cool and damp, not the dry, poisonous gases of a sealed cave she's been warned about, so she guesses there must be some source of fresh air.

21   Feeling nervous and slightly guilty, Alice wraps the buckle in a handkerchief and pushes it into her pocket, then cautiously steps forward.

22   As she moves further in, she feels the chill air curl around her bare legs and arms like a cat. She is walking downhill. She can feel the ground sloping away beneath her feet, uneven and gritty. The scrunch of the stones and gravel is loud in the confined, hushed space. She is aware of the daylight getting fainter and fainter at her back, the further and deeper she goes.

23   Abruptly, she does not want to go on.

Adapted from the novel "Labyrinth" by Kate Mosse

[END OF PASSAGE]

[BLANK PAGE]

FOR OFFICIAL USE

Total
Mark

0860/404

NATIONAL
QUALIFICATIONS
2009

FRIDAY, 8 MAY
1.00 PM – 1.50 PM

ENGLISH
STANDARD GRADE
General Level
Reading
Questions

Fill in these boxes and read what is printed below.

Full name of centre

Town

Forename(s)

Surname

Date of birth
Day Month Year

Scottish candidate number

Number of seat

NB Before leaving the examination room you must give this booklet to the invigilator. If you do not, you may lose all the marks for this paper.

Marks

QUESTIONS

Write your answers in the spaces provided.

Look at Paragraphs 1 and 2.

1. What activity is Alice involved in?

   _____   2 ■ 0

2. "Insects are an occupational hazard . . . " (Paragraph 2)

   Explain **in your own words** what this means.

   _____

   _____   2 1 0

Look at Paragraphs 3 to 5.

3. Write down **three** things the writer tells us in Paragraph 3 which show that it is a hot day.

   (i) _____

   (ii) _____

   (iii) _____   2 1 0

4. How does the writer emphasise that "It's hard work"? (Paragraph 4)

   (*a*) by sentence structure

   _____   2 ■ 0

   (*b*) by word choice

   _____   2 ■ 0

5. Write down an expression from the passage which suggests the hard work has not been worth it so far.

   _____   2 ■ 0

PAGE
TOTAL

Marks

6. "Alice is tempted to go down and join her colleagues." (Paragraph 5)

Give **two** reasons why she is tempted to do this.

(i) _____

(ii) _____ 2 | 1 | 0

Look at Paragraph 7.

7. Tick (✓) the appropriate box to show whether the following statements about Alice are True, False or Cannot Tell from the passage.

	True	False	Cannot Tell			
She wants to show that she can do the job herself.				2	■	0
She does not like her colleagues.				2	■	0
She wants to share her discovery.				2	■	0

Look at Paragraph 10.

8. In Paragraph 10, the writer shows Alice's **feelings** and **thoughts** as she pushes her hand into the soil.

(*a*) **Write down one** expression which shows her **feelings** at this point.

_____ 2 | ■ | 0

(*b*) **Write down one** expression which shows her **thoughts** at this point.

_____ 2 | ■ | 0

9. Why does the writer repeat the word "slowly" in Paragraph 10?

_____ 2 | ■ | 0

[Turn over

PAGE TOTAL

Look at Paragraphs 11 and 12.

10. Alice is "captivated" by the buckle she has found. (Paragraph 11)

    Write down **one** other word from the next paragraph (Paragraph 12) which **also** shows how interested she is in the buckle.

    2 ■ (

11. Give **two** reasons why Alice does not move out of the way of the boulder until the last moment.

    (i) _____

    (ii) _____

    2 1

12. Explain carefully what is surprising about the word "gracefully" in Paragraph 12.

    _____

    2 1

Look at Paragraphs 13 to 16.

13. " . . . dirt, dizzy and disorientated." (Paragraph 13)

    Identify the **technique** used here.

    _____

    2 ■ (

14. **In your own words**, explain why Alice "turns cold". (Paragraph 13)

    _____

    _____

    2 1

15. Why do you think Alice does **not** "call out to attract someone's attention"? (Paragraph 15)

    _____

    _____

    2 1

PAGE
TOTAL

Marks

Look at Paragraphs 17 to 19.

16. ". . . the stone had stood guard." (Paragraph 17)

Give **two** reasons why this expression is appropriate.

(i) _____

(ii) _____   2 1 0

17. "Slowly, her eyes become accustomed to the gloom." (Paragraph 19)

Explain how the writer develops this idea in the next sentence.

_____

_____   2 1 0

Look at Paragraph 21 to the end of the passage.

18. As Alice steps into the tunnel, she experiences **two** feelings. **In your own words**, explain what these **two** feelings are.

(i) _____

(ii) _____   2 1 0

19. "Abruptly, she does not want to go on." (Paragraph 23)

Give **two** reasons why this is an effective ending to the passage.

(i) _____

(ii) _____   2 1 0

[Turn over

PAGE
TOTAL

Marks

Think about the passage as a whole.

20. The writer has written this story in the present tense.

Why do you think the writer has done this?

_____ 2 ■ 0

21. What do you think will happen next in the story?

Tick (✓) the answer which you think is most likely.

Alice will return to her colleagues.	
Alice will go further into the cave and make an exciting discovery.	
Alice will be trapped in the cave.	

Give **two** pieces of evidence from the passage to support your answer.

(i) _____

(ii) _____ 2 1 0

[*END OF QUESTION PAPER*]

PAGE
TOTAL

FOR OFFICIAL USE

p2	
p3	
p4	
p5	
p6	
TOTAL MARK	

FOR OFFICIAL USE

[BLANK PAGE]

STANDARD GRADE | CREDIT

2009
READING

[BLANK PAGE]

C

0860/405

| NATIONAL QUALIFICATIONS 2009 | FRIDAY, 8 MAY 2.30 PM – 3.20 PM | ENGLISH STANDARD GRADE Credit Level Reading Text |

Read carefully the passage overleaf. It will help if you read it twice. When you have done so, answer the questions. Use the spaces provided in the Question/Answer booklet.

In the following passage, taken from a novel, the narrator, Christopher, has a frightening experience.

1   It was a sunny, windy morning. I remember watching from the playroom windows the leaves blowing in the front yard over the carriage track. Uncle Philip had been downstairs with my mother since shortly after breakfast, and I had been able to relax for a while, believing as I did that nothing could happen to her while he was with her.

2   Then midway through the morning I heard Uncle Philip calling me. I went out on to the landing and, looking down over the balcony rail, saw my mother and Uncle Philip standing in the hall, gazing up at me. For the first time in weeks I sensed something cheerful about them, as though they had just been enjoying a joke. The front door was ajar and a long streak of sunlight was falling across the hall. Uncle Philip said:

3   "Look here, Christopher. You're always saying you want a piano accordion. Well, I intend to buy you one. I spotted an excellent one in a window in Hankow Road yesterday. I propose the two of us go and look it over. If it takes your fancy, then it's yours. Good plan?"

4   This brought me down the staircase at great speed. I jumped the last four steps and circled round the adults, flapping my arms in impersonation of a bird of prey. As I did so, to my delight, I heard my mother laughing; laughing in a way I had not heard her laugh for a while. In fact it is possible it was this very atmosphere—this feeling that things were perhaps starting to return to what they had been—which played a significant part in causing me to "lower my guard". I asked Uncle Philip when we could go, to which he shrugged and said:

5   "Why not now? If we leave it, someone else might spot it. Perhaps someone's buying it at this moment, even as we speak!"

6   I rushed to the doorway and again my mother laughed. Then she told me I would have to put on proper shoes and a jacket. I remember thinking of protesting about the jacket, but then deciding not to in case the adults changed their minds, not only about the accordion, but also about this whole light-hearted mood we were enjoying.

7   I waved casually to my mother as Uncle Philip and I set off across the front courtyard. Then several steps on, as I was hurrying towards the waiting carriage, Uncle Philip grasped me by the shoulder, saying: "Look! Wave to your mother!" despite my already having done so. But I thought nothing of it at the time, and turning as bidden, waved once more to my mother's figure, elegantly upright in the doorway.

8   For much of the way, the carriage followed the route my mother and I usually took to the city centre. Uncle Philip was quiet, which surprised me a little, but I assumed this was perhaps his normal custom on a journey. Whenever I pointed out to him anything we were passing, he would reply cheerfully enough; but the next moment he would be staring silently once more out at the view. The leafy boulevards gave way to the narrow crowded streets, and our driver began to shout at the rickshaws and pedestrians in our path. As we approached the vegetable market, Uncle Philip suddenly rapped his cane to make the carriage stop.

9   "From here, we'll go on foot," he said to me. "I know a good short cut. It'll be much quicker."

10   This made perfectly good sense. I knew from experience how the little streets off Nanking Road could become so clogged with people that a carriage or motor car would often not move for five, even ten minutes at a time. I thus allowed him to help me down from the carriage with no argument. But it was then, I recall, that I had my

first presentiment that something was wrong. Perhaps it was something in Uncle Philip's manner. But then he smiled and made some remark I did not catch in the noise around us. He pointed towards a nearby alley and I stayed close behind him as we pushed our way through the good-humoured throng. We moved from bright sun to shade, and then he stopped and turned to me, right there in the midst of the jostling crowd. Placing a hand on my shoulder, he asked:

11   "Christopher, do you know where we are now? Can you guess?"

12   I looked around me. Then pointing towards a stone arch under which crowds were pressing around the vegetable stalls, I replied: "Yes. That's Kiukiang Road through there."

13   "Ah. So you know exactly where we are." He gave an odd laugh. "You know your way around here very well."

14   I nodded and waited, the feeling rising from the pit of my stomach that something of great horror was about to unfold. Perhaps Uncle Philip was about to say something else—perhaps he had planned the whole thing quite differently—but at that moment, as we stood there jostled on all sides, I believe he saw in my face that the game was up. A terrible confusion passed across his features, then he said, barely audibly in the din:

15   "Good boy."

16   He grasped my shoulder again and let his gaze wander about him. Then he appeared to come to a decision I had already anticipated.

17   "Good boy!" he said, this time more loudly, his voice trembling with emotion. Then he added: "I didn't want you hurt. You understand that? I didn't want you hurt."

18   With that he spun round and vanished into the crowd. I made a half-hearted effort to follow, and after a moment caught sight of his white jacket hurrying through the people. Then he had passed under the arch and out of my view.

19   For the next few moments I remained standing there in the crowd, trying not to pursue the logic of what had just occurred. Then suddenly I began to move, back in the direction we had just come, to the street in which we had left the carriage. Abandoning all sense of decorum, I forced my way through the crowds, sometimes pushing violently, sometimes squeezing myself through gaps, so that people laughed or called angrily after me. I reached the street to discover of course that the carriage had long since gone on its way. For a few confused seconds I stood in the middle of the street, trying to form in my head a map of my route back home. I then began to run as fast as I could.

20   I set off at a run down that long road, and even though I soon began to pant pathetically, even though the heat and exhaustion reduced me at times to little more than walking pace, I believe I did not stop at all.

21   I knew as soon as I turned through our gateway—though there was nothing obvious to tell me so—that I was too late. I found the front door bolted. I ran to the back door, which opened for me, and ran through the house shouting.

22   The house appeared to be empty. And I knew, as I had known throughout that punishing run home, that my mother was gone.

Adapted from the novel *When We Were Orphans* by Kazuo Ishiguro

[END OF PASSAGE]

[BLANK PAGE]

FOR OFFICIAL USE

C

Total Mark

0860/406

NATIONAL
QUALIFICATIONS
2009

FRIDAY, 8 MAY
2.30 PM – 3.20 PM

ENGLISH
STANDARD GRADE
Credit Level
Reading
Questions

Fill in these boxes and read what is printed below.

Full name of centre

Town

Forename(s)

Surname

Date of birth
   Day   Month   Year

Scottish candidate number

Number of seat

NB Before leaving the examination room you must give this booklet to the invigilator.
If you do not, you may lose all the marks for this paper.

SA 0860/406 6/42520

Marks

QUESTIONS

Write your answers in the spaces provided.

Look at Paragraphs 1 and 2.

1. "I had been able to relax for a while" (Paragraph 1)

   (*a*) Why was Christopher able to relax?

   His uncle was downstairs with his mother 2 ①

   (*b*) What does the expression "for a while" suggest about Christopher's usual state of mind?

   It is hectic, busy ②

2. Write down an expression from Paragraph 2 which suggests that the family had been under strain for some time.

   First time in weeks something cheerful ②

Look at Paragraphs 3 to 6.

3. Uncle Philip seemed at first to be a generous and caring person.

   What evidence is there in this section that he was **both** generous and caring?

   "I intend to buy you one"
   He wants to buy Chris an accordian ② 1

4. Christopher became very excited about Uncle Philip's plan.

   Give **three** ways in which the writer indicates Christopher's excitement in Paragraph 4.

   (i) _dashes_

   (ii) _simile_

   (iii) _list_ 2 1

PAGE
TOTAL

Marks

5. Why do you think Christopher was delighted to hear his mother laugh?
   (Paragraph 4)

   ~~She~~ They had been through tough times where she obviously hasnt laughed

   2 (1) 0

6. Explain the function of the dashes in ". . . this very atmosphere—this feeling that things were perhaps starting to return to what they had been—which played . . ."
   (Paragraph 4)

   It adds extra info about his thoughts

   (2) 1 0

7. **In your own words**, explain what Christopher means by "lower my guard".
   (Paragraph 4)

   He means he began to stop worrying.

   (2) ■ 0

8. Give **two** reasons why Christopher did not object to wearing a jacket.

   (i) He did not want to dampen the mood

   (ii) He didn't want to put the adults ~~off~~ buffing the accordian

   (2) 1 0

Look at Paragraph 7.

9. Give **two** pieces of evidence which might suggest that Uncle Philip was feeling tense.

   (i) The fact he graspeed his shoulder

   (ii) They were hurrying

   2 (1) 0

[Turn over

PAGE TOTAL

Marks

10. "But I thought nothing of it at the time" (Paragraph 7)

What does this statement suggest?

It turns out bad later on.
It is significant

2 ■

Look at Paragraphs 8 and 9.

11. What explanation does Christopher suggest for his uncle's silences on their journey? (Paragraph 8)

Use your own words in your answer.

It was the usual way he behaved on a journey

2 1

12. **In your own words**, explain how the writer indicates the changing surroundings along the route towards the city centre.

The open green subburbs made way to slim streets

2 1

13. "From here, we'll go on foot . . ." (Paragraph 9)

From your reading of the passage as a whole, what was the real reason for Uncle Philip's decision to leave the carriage and start walking?

To get him on his own

■

Look at Paragraph 10.

14. Quote **three** examples of effective word choice used by the writer to describe the busy streets "off Nanking Road".

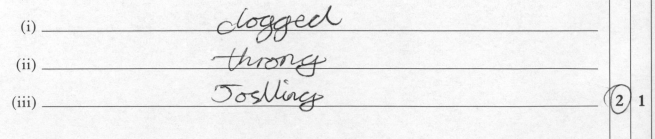

(i) *clogged*

(ii) *throng*

(iii) *Jostling*

2 1

PAGE
TOTA

Marks

15. "We moved from bright sun to shade" (Paragraph 10)

Why do you think the writer refers to **light** and **darkness** at this point in the passage?

to represent the change in his uncle

2 (1) 0

Look at Paragraphs 14 to 17.

16. The writer describes the strong feelings experienced by both Christopher and Uncle Philip.

(*a*)   Quote **two** expressions which show Christopher's strong feelings.

pit of my stomach
great horror

(2) 1 0

(*b*)   Quote **two** expressions which show Uncle Philip's strong feelings.

I didn't want to hurt you
Good boy

2 1 (0)

17. Why did Uncle Philip repeat "I didn't want you hurt"? (Paragraph 17)

to emphasize it

(2) ■ 0

[Turn over

PAGE
TOTAL

Marks

Look at Paragraph 19.

18. "Then suddenly I began to move . . ." (Paragraph 19)

    Comment on the writer's use of word choice **and** sentence structure in this paragraph to describe Christopher's journey back.

    (*a*) Word choice:

    There is lots of verbs to describe his movement also aggresive languge to show his emergencs   ② 1

    (*b*) Sentence structure:

    Long sentences to convey the length and things he had to do.   ② 1

19. "all sense of decorum" (Paragraph 19)

    Tick (✓) the box beside the best definition of "decorum".

proper behaviour	✓
bad behaviour	
anxious behaviour	
aggressive behaviour	

    ② ■

Look at Paragraph 20 to the end of the passage.

20. In Paragraph 20, the writer describes Christopher as physically tired but mentally determined. Give **one** piece of evidence showing he was tired and **one** piece of evidence showing his determination.

    exhausted ~~pathetically~~ pant

    I Believe   2 ①

PAGE
TOTA

Marks

21. "I knew as soon as . . ." (Paragraph 21)
    "I knew, as I had known . . ." (Paragraph 22)

    Why does the writer repeat "I knew" in this way?

    The repetition highlights his knowing ② ■ 0

Think about the passage as a whole.

22. Explain what you think happened to Christopher's mother.

    Support your answer by referring to evidence from the passage.

    Explanation *His mother was taken to a home or hospital*

    Evidence *"The doors were bolted up"*   2 ① 0

[END OF QUESTION PAPER]

37

50

FOR OFFICIAL USE

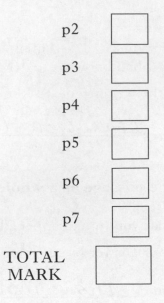

p2

p3

p4

p5

p6

p7

TOTAL
MARK

FOR OFFICIAL USE

STANDARD GRADE | FOUNDATION | GENERAL | CREDIT

2006
WRITING

[BLANK PAGE]

F G C

0860/407

NATIONAL QUALIFICATIONS 2006	WEDNESDAY, 3 MAY 9.00 AM – 10.15 AM	**ENGLISH STANDARD GRADE** Foundation, General and Credit Levels Writing

Read This First

1   Inside this booklet, there are photographs and words.
Use them to help you when you are thinking about what to write.
Look at all the material and think about all the possibilities.

2   There are 21 assignments altogether for you to choose from.

3   Decide which assignment you are going to attempt.
Choose only **one** and write its number in the margin of your answer book.

4   Pay close attention to what you are asked to write.
Plan what you are going to write.
Read and check your work before you hand it in.
Any changes to your work should be made clearly.

SCOTTISH QUALIFICATIONS AUTHORITY

©

FIRST **Look at the picture opposite.**
It shows a couple parting.

NEXT Think how you might feel about leaving someone you care for.

WHAT YOU HAVE TO WRITE

1. **Write about** a time when you were separated from someone you cared about.

   You should concentrate on your **thoughts and feelings**.

   OR

2. **Write a short story** using the title:

   Never Forgotten.

   OR

3. We should be less afraid to speak openly about our feelings.
   Discuss.

   OR

4. **Write in any way you choose** using the picture opposite as your inspiration.

[Turn over

FIRST   **Look at the picture opposite.**
                   It shows a lightning strike.

NEXT   Think about the power of storms.

WHAT YOU HAVE TO WRITE

5. **Describe** both the excitement and the fear you experienced when you were caught in a storm.

   OR

6. **Write a short story** using **ONE** of the following titles:

   Stormchaser   Lightning Strikes Twice.

   OR

7. **Write a newspaper article** with the following headline:

   Storm Causes Widespread Damage.

   OR

8. Weather plays an important part in our everyday lives.
   Give your views.

[Turn over

FIRST   **Look at the picture opposite.**
                 It shows a group of students.

NEXT   Think about life during and after school.

WHAT YOU HAVE TO WRITE

9. **Giving reasons**, write about your plans for when you leave school.

   OR

10. **Write a short story** using the following title:

    The Examination.

    OR

11. **Write an article** for your school magazine in which you describe the high points **and** the low points of your school years.

    OR

12. New places, new faces.

    Write about a time when you had to cope with new people in new surroundings.

    Remember to include your **thoughts and feelings**.

[Turn over

FIRST   **Look at the picture opposite.**
         It shows a traffic jam.

NEXT   Think about travel problems.

WHAT YOU HAVE TO WRITE

---

13. **Write about** an occasion when you were delayed during a journey.
    You should concentrate on your **thoughts and feelings**.

    OR

14. **Write a short story** using the following title:
    The Road to Nowhere.

    OR

15. Road rage, air rage—the modern age.
    Life today is simply too stressful.
    Discuss.

[Turn over

FIRST   **Look at the picture opposite.**
             It shows a young couple who have fallen out.

NEXT   Think about relationships.

WHAT YOU HAVE TO WRITE
---

16. **Write a short story** using **ONE** of the following openings:

    EITHER

    Jill stared ahead intently, always away from him, focused firmly on the wall. He tried to speak. She raised her arm in protest . . .

    OR

    Andrew didn't know what to do. Just hours earlier things had been simply perfect. Now this. He let his mind wander back to . . .

    OR

17. Magazines for young people do more good than harm.

    Give your views.

    OR

18. **Write about** your **thoughts and feelings** at a time when you were aware that someone simply wasn't listening.

[Turn over for assignments 19 to 21 on *Page twelve*

There are no pictures for these assignments.

19. **Write a short story** using the following opening.

    "He awoke in the ashes of a dead city. The cruel sun glared, showing neither pity nor mercy. He shook himself. It was no dream."

    Make sure that you develop **character** and **setting** as well as **plot**.

    OR

20. Look at me!

    Is it more important to be an individual or to fit in with the crowd?

    Discuss.

    OR

21. **Write a short story** using the title:

    Out of Time.

    Make sure that you develop **character** and **setting** as well as **plot**.

[END OF QUESTION PAPER]

STANDARD GRADE | FOUNDATION | GENERAL | CREDIT

2007
WRITING

[BLANK PAGE]

FGC

0860/407

NATIONAL
QUALIFICATIONS
2007

TUESDAY, 1 MAY
9.00 AM – 10.15 AM

ENGLISH
STANDARD GRADE
Foundation, General
and Credit Levels
Writing

Read This First

1   Inside this booklet, there are photographs and words.
    Use them to help you when you are thinking about what to write.
    Look at all the material and think about all the possibilities.

2   There are 23 assignments altogether for you to choose from.

3   Decide which assignment you are going to attempt.
    Choose only **one** and write its number in the margin of your answer book.

4   Pay close attention to what you are asked to write.
    Plan what you are going to write.
    Read and check your work before you hand it in.
    Any changes to your work should be made clearly.

SCOTTISH
QUALIFICATIONS
AUTHORITY

©

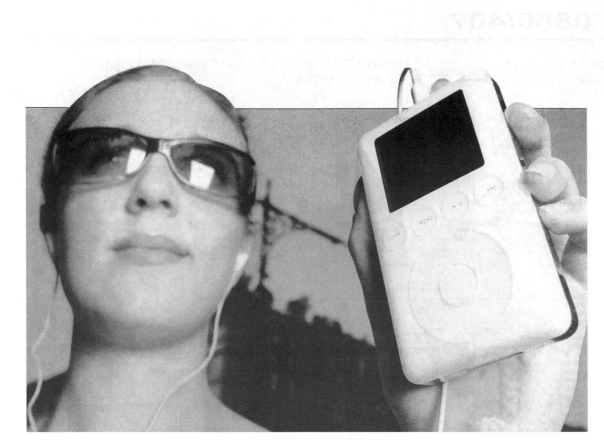

FIRST   **Look at the picture opposite.**
         It shows a young woman with an MP3 player.

NEXT   Think about the importance of technology.

WHAT YOU HAVE TO WRITE

---

1. The one piece of technology I couldn't live without.

   Write about the importance to you of **ONE** piece of technology.

   OR

2. Young people today care too much for personal possessions.
   Give your views.

   OR

3. **Write a short story** using **ONE** of the following titles:

   Futureshock   She Saw the Future.

   You should develop **setting** and **character** as well as **plot**.

                                                        [Turn over

FIRST   **Look at the picture opposite.
It shows a young boy being led by his mother.**

NEXT   Think about your schooldays.

WHAT YOU HAVE TO WRITE

4. School Memories.

    Write about a person, place, or incident from your schooldays which you find unforgettable.

    Remember to include your **thoughts and feelings**.

    OR

5. **Write a short story** using the following opening:

    The reluctance was written all over John's face. He tugged at his mother's hand. He winced. He grimaced. He complained. Still his mother led him on . . .

    You should develop **setting** and **character** as well as **plot**.

    OR

6. All pupils should wear school uniform.

    Give your views.

[Turn over

FIRST   **Look at the picture opposite.**
             It shows a lake in winter.

NEXT   Think about special places.

WHAT YOU HAVE TO WRITE
---

7.   Sometimes a special place can inspire us.

     Write about such a place.

     Remember to include your **thoughts and feelings**.

     OR

8.   **Write in any way you choose** using the picture opposite as your
     inspiration.

     OR

9.   **Write about** a time when you were alone but happy.

     You should concentrate on your **thoughts and feelings**.

     OR

10. **Write an informative article** for a travel magazine titled:

     The Best Holiday Destination For Young People.

                                                              [Turn over

FIRST   **Look at the picture opposite.**
                It shows a man under pressure.

NEXT   Think about the pressures of life.

WHAT YOU HAVE TO WRITE

---

11. **Write about** a time in your life when you had to face personal pressure.

    You should describe your **thoughts and feelings**.

    OR

12. **Write a short story** using **ONE** of the following titles:

    The Underdog   Free at Last.

    You should develop **setting** and **character** as well as **plot**.

    OR

13. It's Just Not Fair!

    Write about an occasion when you took a stand against injustice.

    You should concentrate on your **thoughts and feelings** as well as what you did.

    OR

14. These days young people are unfairly treated by the media.

    Give your views.

    [Turn over

FIRST **Look at the picture opposite.**
It shows a young woman on a bus, alone with her thoughts.

NEXT Think about moments of reflection.

> WHAT YOU HAVE TO WRITE

15. "The glass is always half full; never half empty."

It is important to have a positive outlook on life.

Give your views.

OR

16. **Write about** an occasion when you had an unpleasant duty to perform.

You should concentrate on your **thoughts and feelings**.

OR

17. Act Your Age!

There are fewer chances today simply to be yourself.

Give your views.

OR

18. **Write a short story** using **ONE** of the following titles:

Stranger in a Strange Land   No Return.

You should develop **setting** and **character** as well as **plot**.

[Turn over for assignments 19 to 23 on *Page twelve*

There are no pictures for these assignments.

19. We should try to solve the problems here on earth before we spend more on space exploration.

    Give your views.

    OR

20. **Describe the scene** brought to mind by the following:

    A stark land of leafless trees and merciless wind.

    OR

21. We forget our past at our peril!

    Not enough is being done to keep Scottish heritage alive.

    Write a newspaper article in which you give your views on this topic.

    OR

22. There are special times of the year when people celebrate in their own way.

    Describe such a special time, bringing out its importance to you, your family, and your community.

    OR

23. **Write a short story** using the following title:

    The Traveller.

    You should develop **setting** and **character** as well as **plot**.

[END OF QUESTION PAPER]

STANDARD GRADE | FOUNDATION | GENERAL | CREDIT

2008
WRITING

[BLANK PAGE]

F G C

0860/407

NATIONAL
QUALIFICATIONS
2008

TUESDAY, 6 MAY
9.00 AM – 10.15 AM

ENGLISH
STANDARD GRADE
Foundation, General
and Credit Levels
Writing

Read This First

1   Inside this booklet, there are photographs and words.
    Use them to help you when you are thinking about what to write.
    Look at all the material and think about all the possibilities.

2   There are 22 assignments altogether for you to choose from.

3   Decide which assignment you are going to attempt.
    Choose only **one** and write its number in the margin of your answer book.

4   Pay close attention to what you are asked to write.
    Plan what you are going to write.
    Read and check your work before you hand it in.
    Any changes to your work should be made clearly.

SA 0860/407 6/20600

FIRST   **Look at the picture opposite.**
                 It shows a car in heavy rain and hail.

NEXT   Think about the dangers of extreme weather.

> ## WHAT YOU HAVE TO WRITE

1. **Write a short story** using the following opening:

    The car skidded violently. He struggled to regain control. Close to panic, he wrenched the steering wheel to the right . . .

    You should develop **setting** and **character** as well as **plot**.

    OR

2. What's going on with our weather?

    Individuals need to take steps to tackle climate change.

    Give your views.

    OR

3. Journeys can take unexpected turns.

    Write about an occasion when this happened to **you**.

    Remember to include your **thoughts and feelings**.

[Turn over

FIRST   **Look at the picture opposite.**
           It shows young people together in a school cafeteria.

NEXT   Think about school experiences.

WHAT YOU HAVE TO WRITE
---

4. A Best Friend Should Be . . .

    Write about the ideal qualities of a best friend.

    OR

5. Youth culture. There's no such thing.

    Give your views.

    OR

6. **Write about** an occasion when your loyalty to a friend was pushed
    to the limit.

    Remember to include your **thoughts and feelings**.

    OR

7. **Write a short story** using the following title:

    The School Gate.

    You should develop **setting** and **character** as well as **plot**.

                                                              [Turn over

[0860/407]

FIRST   **Look at the picture opposite.
It shows a man staring.**

NEXT   Think about being observed.

WHAT YOU HAVE TO WRITE

---

8. Big Brother is Watching You!

   Write about an occasion when you felt that there was no escape from authority.

   Remember to include your **thoughts and feelings**.

   OR

9. **Write a short story** using **ONE** of the following titles:

   Seeing is Believing   Close Up

   You should develop **setting** and **character** as well as **plot**.

   OR

10. All You Need is an Audience.

    The media give young people the idea that success comes easily.

    Give your views.

[Turn over

FIRST   **Look at the picture opposite.
It shows a boy with his grandfather.**

NEXT   Think about the positive relationship you have with an older
relative.

WHAT YOU HAVE TO WRITE

11. **Write about** an occasion when you learned a valuable lesson from
an older relative.

Remember to include your **thoughts and feelings**.

OR

12. **Write a short story** using the following opening:

Those were the moments he loved most. Grandpa reading to him
with that lilting voice telling stories of . . .

You should develop **setting** and **character** as well as **plot**.

OR

13. We do not give the older generation the respect they deserve.

Give your views.

OR

14. **Write in any way you choose** using the picture opposite as your
inspiration.

[Turn over

FIRST   **Look at the picture opposite.**
                It shows an aircraft in the sunset.

NEXT   Think about air travel.

WHAT YOU HAVE TO WRITE

---

15. The damage to the environment caused by aircraft outweighs the advantages of cheap air travel.

    Give your views.

    OR

16. **Write a short story** using **ONE** of the following titles:

    A New Beginning   Touchdown

    You should develop **setting** and **character** as well as **plot**.

    OR

17. **Write in any way you choose** using the picture opposite as your inspiration.

[Turn over for assignments 18 to 22 on *Page twelve*

There are no pictures for these assignments.

18. **Write an informative article** for your school magazine titled:

    Technology: the impact on my education.

    OR

19. Nowadays there is less freedom of choice.

    Give your views.

    OR

20. **Write a short story** with the following opening:

    Beth stared again at the square glow from the computer screen in disbelief. She was going to be reunited with her sister at long last. She could hardly wait . . .

    You should develop **setting** and **character** as well as **plot**.

    OR

21. Education is about what we learn both **inside** and **outside** the classroom.

    Give your views.

    OR

22. **Describe the scene** brought to mind by **ONE** of the following:

    EITHER

    Snow fell, the flimsiest drops of geometric perfection, lightly, gently onto the village rooftops.

    OR

    With merciless rage, the sun scorched the earth to brittle hardness.

[END OF QUESTION PAPER]

STANDARD GRADE | FOUNDATION | GENERAL | CREDIT

2009
WRITING

[BLANK PAGE]

F G C

0860/407

NATIONAL
QUALIFICATIONS
2009

FRIDAY, 8 MAY
9.00 AM – 10.15 AM

ENGLISH
STANDARD GRADE
Foundation, General
and Credit Levels
Writing

Read This First

1   Inside this booklet, there are photographs and words.
    Use them to help you when you are thinking about what to write.
    Look at all the material and think about all the possibilities.

2   There are 21 assignments altogether for you to choose from.

3   Decide which assignment you are going to attempt.
    Choose only **one** and write its number in the margin of your answer book.

4   Pay close attention to what you are asked to write.
    Plan what you are going to write.
    Read and check your work before you hand it in.
    Any changes to your work should be made clearly.

FIRST   **Look at the picture opposite.**
         It shows a statue overlooking a city.

NEXT   Think about life in a city.

WHAT YOU HAVE TO WRITE
---

1. **Write about an occasion** when you went on a school trip to a city.

   Remember to include your **thoughts and feelings**.

   OR

2. Holidays are not just about sun, sea and sand.

   Give your views.

   OR

3. **Write a short story** using the following opening:

   From a great height he watched. Cars, buses, boats, people. Slowly, he drew his plans . . .

   You should develop **setting** and **character** as well as **plot**.

   OR

4. **Write in any way you choose** using the picture opposite as your inspiration.

[Turn over

FIRST   **Look at the pictures opposite.**
                    They show people involved in different sports.

NEXT   Think about what sport means to you.

| WHAT YOU HAVE TO WRITE |
---

5. My Sporting Hero.

   Write a magazine article giving information about your favourite sportsperson.

   OR

6. There should be more opportunities for sport in local communities.

   Give your views.

   OR

7. **Write a short story** using the title:

   Against the Odds

   You should develop **setting** and **character** as well as **plot**.

   OR

8. **Write about** a sporting occasion when taking part was more important than winning.

   Remember to include your **thoughts and feelings**.

[Turn over

Page six

FIRST   **Look at the picture opposite.
It shows a tigress and her cubs.**

NEXT   Think about protecting animals.

WHAT YOU HAVE TO WRITE

9. One of the Family.

   Write about the importance of a pet in your life.

   Remember to include your **thoughts and feelings**.

   OR

10. **Write a magazine article** in which you present the case **for** the protection of an animal in danger.

   OR

11. **Write a short story** using **ONE** of the following titles:

   The Animal Kingdom   Animal Magic

   You should develop **setting** and **character** as well as **plot**.

   [Turn over

Page eight

FIRST   **Look at the picture opposite.**
             It shows a man at the top of a staircase.

NEXT   Think about achievements in your life.

WHAT YOU HAVE TO WRITE

12. **Write about** an occasion when you achieved a personal goal after a struggle.

    Remember to include your **thoughts and feelings**.

    OR

13. Achievement in school is about more than success in exams.

    Give your views.

    OR

14. **Write a short story** using the following opening:

    It had been tough. Sacrifice. Time. Effort. Now she had succeeded. Let the new life begin . . .

    You should develop **setting** and **character** as well as **plot**.

                                                                    [Turn over

[0860/407]

FIRST   **Look at the picture opposite.**
         It shows two people on a survival course.

NEXT   Think about outdoor activities.

WHAT YOU HAVE TO WRITE

---

15. **Write about** an occasion when you learned new skills through taking part in an outdoor activity.

    Remember to include your **thoughts and feelings**.

    OR

16. **Write a short story** using the following title:

    Trapped in the Forest

    You should develop **setting** and **character** as well as **plot**.

    OR

17. Outdoor education should be available to all pupils.

    Give your views.

[Turn over for assignments 18 to 21 on *Page twelve*

There are no pictures for these assignments.

18. **Describe the scene** brought to mind by **ONE** of the following:

    Light as air, they hovered then swooped, twisting impossibly around feather clouds.

    OR

    Waves lapped at pebbles on the distant shore and a kindly sun drew a gentle haze over the land.

19. Holidays at home are better for the environment than going abroad.

    Give your views.

    OR

20. **Write about** an occasion when you were a positive role model for a friend or relative.

    Remember to include your **thoughts and feelings**.

    OR

21. **Write a short story** using the following title:

    Paradise Lost

    You should develop **setting** and **character** as well as **plot**.

[END OF QUESTION PAPER]

[BLANK PAGE]

[BLANK PAGE]

[BLANK PAGE]

Acknowledgements

Permission has been sought from all relevant copyright holders and Bright Red Publishing is grateful for the use of the following:

Extract from 'You Don't Know Me' by David Klass. Reprinted with permission from The Aaron M. Priest Literary Agency, 2009 (2006 General Close Reading pages 2 & 3);

An extract from the article 'Casting a spell all over America' by Alex Massie, taken from The Scotsman, Tuesday 8 June 2004 (2006 Credit Close Reading page 2);

The photograph '7th Scripps Howard Spelling Bee Enters Final Rounds' © Matthew Cavanaugh/Getty Images (2006 Credit Close Reading page 2);

A photograph of lightning taken from www.sydneystormchasers.com © James Harris (2006 F/G/C Writing page 4);

The photograph, 'Scots will be squeezed out "Fee Refugees!"' by David Moir, taken from The Scotsman, 26 August 2004 © The Scotsman Publications Ltd (2006 F/G/C Writing page 6);

The photograph, 'Stretching the Nerves' by Kieran Dodds © Herald & Times Group (2006 F/G/C Writing page 8);

The photograph 'People' © Design Pics/Alamy Limited (2006 F/G/C Writing page 10);

Article adapted from 'The Fabulous Biker Boys (and Girls)' by John Dodd taken from the Sunday Telegraph Magazine © Telegraph Media Group (28 August 2005) (2007 General Close Reading page 2);

An extract from 'Findings' by Kathleen Jamie. Published by Sort of Books (2007 Credit Close Reading pages 2 & 3);

The photograph, 'iPod Generation' © Dan Callister/RexFeatures (2007 F/G/C Writing page 2);

A photograph © Hulton Archive/Getty (2007 F/G/C Writing page 4);

A photograph © www.danheller.com (2007 F/G/C Writing page 6);

A picture © Hashim Akib (2007 F/G/C Writing page 8);

A photograph © David Hogsholt/Reportage by Getty Images (2007 F/G/C Writing page 10);

The article 'Saddle the white horses' by Dave Flanagan, taken from The Herald magazine 22 April 2006 (2008 General Close Reading page 2);

An extract from 'Atonement' by Ian McEwan, published by Jonathan Cape. Reprinted by permission of The Random House Group (2008 Credit Close Reading pages 2 & 3);

A photograph taken from www.bigfoto.com (2008 F/G/C Writing page 2);

The photograph 'Chips are down' by Robert Perry taken from Scotland on Sunday, 2 July 2006 © The Scotsman Publications Ltd (2008 F/G/C Writing page 4);

The photograph 'Eye Opener' © Steve Double (2008 F/G/C Writing page 6);

The photograph 'Airbus 320' by Ian Britton. Reproduced with permission of Freefoto.com (2008 F/G/C Writing page 10);

An extract from 'Labyrinth' by Kate Mosse, published by Orion Books (2005) (2009 General Close Reading pages 2 & 3);

An extract from 'When We Were Orphans' by Kazuo Ishiguro, published by Faber and Faber (2009 Credit Close Reading pages 2 & 3);

A photograph taken from www.bigfoto.com (2009 F/G/C Writing page 2);

A photograph © FRANCK FIFE/AFP/Getty Images (2009 F/G/C Writing page 4);

A photograph by Phil Wilkinson © The Scotsman Publications Ltd (2009 F/G/C Writing page 4);

The photograph 'Surfing. Saltburn by the Sea, Yorkshire' by Ian Britton. Reproduced with permission of Freefoto.com (2009 F/G/C Writing page 4);

A photograph of a girl ski-ing © Neil McQuoid (2009 F/G/C Writing page 4);

The photograph, 'Supermum Tigress licks her new cubs in Hongshan Zoo in Nanjing, China' © Herald & Times Group (2009 F/G/C Writing page 6);

A photograph © Blackout Concepts/Alamy (2009 F/G/C Writing page 8);

The photograph 'I will survive: Learning to make fire without matches is a basic bushcraft skill © Roger Bamber/Alamy (2009 F/G/C Writing page 10).